T0417727

B!TCH, STOP! PLEASE....

www.amplifypublishinggroup.com

Bitch, Stop! Please . . . : An Entrepreneur's Journey of Innovation, from Chaos to Clarity

For more information, please contact:
Amplify Publishing, an imprint of Amplify Publishing Group
620 Herndon Parkway, Suite 220
Herndon, VA 20170
info@amplifypublishing.com

Library of Congress Control Number: 2024922449

CPSIA Code: PRV0425B

ISBN-13: 979-8-89138-492-7

Printed in the United States

To the bold dreamers and relentless builders, this book is for you—the budding entrepreneurs navigating the stress, doubt, and those moments of overwhelming numbness. May these pages remind you that chaos is part of the journey, but clarity is always within reach. Keep pushing, keep believing, and never let the noise drown out your fire. You've got this.

SHARMIN ALI

B!TCH, STOP! PLEASE...

AN ENTREPRENEUR'S JOURNEY

OF INNOVATION, FROM CHAOS TO CLARITY

amplify

an imprint of Amplify Publishing Group

CONTENTS

A LOVE LETTER TO LIFE

Dear Life,

As I sit down to write this letter, I find myself overwhelmed with a flood of memories, lessons, and experiences that you have gifted me over the past eighteen years. Today, as I celebrate my thirty-sixth birthday, I want to take a moment to reflect on our journey together—from the wide-eyed dreams of an eighteen-year-old to the relentless pursuit of entrepreneurship, and now preparing to share my story with the world.

When I was eighteen, I was brimming with curiosity and ambition. You, dear Life, have been an incredible teacher, guiding me through the highest of highs and the lowest of lows. You've taught me resilience, adaptability, and the importance of perseverance. Each challenge I faced became a stepping stone, each success a reminder of my potential. You showed me that the path to entrepreneurship is not a straight line but a winding road filled with unexpected turns. In my early twenties, I embarked on a journey that took me to the farthest corners of the globe.

From the bustling streets of New York to the serene landscapes of Chile, from the vibrant cultures of Africa to the historic charm of Europe, I immersed myself in the richness of different worlds. Traveling to over seventy countries, I gathered stories, learned from diverse cultures, and opened my mind to endless possibilities. Each destination was a chapter in my life, filled with adventures that broadened my horizons and shaped my entrepreneurial spirit. You, dear Life, have shown me the beauty of human connection. In every country

I visited, I met people who inspired me with their stories of courage and innovation.

From a small village in India where I learned about sustainable farming, to a tech hub in Silicon Valley where I witnessed ground-breaking innovations, every encounter added a new dimension to my understanding of the world and the potential of entrepreneurship. Throughout my travels, I made it a point to journal about my experiences. These journals became my confidants, capturing the essence of my journey, my thoughts, my fears, and my dreams. They are a testament to the incredible ride we've had together, dear Life. It is through these writings that I have decided to compile my experiences into a book—a love letter to you, celebrating the myriad ways you've shaped me into who I am today.

This book is not just a memoir of my travels but a guide for aspiring entrepreneurs. I want to share the lessons you've taught me, the strategies I've developed, and the mindset that has kept me going, no matter the obstacles. My book is a testament to my unstoppable spirit, my unquenchable thirst to make it big in life. I want to show the world that with passion, perseverance, and the willingness to learn, anyone can build their own successful company and bring about meaningful change.

Dear Life, you've taught me that entrepreneurship is about more than just building a business. It's about solving problems, creating value, and making a positive impact on the world. It's about resilience in the face of failure, and the courage to try again. There were times when I faced setbacks, when the startups I built didn't take off as I had hoped. But you were always there, reminding me that failure is not the end but a new beginning—a chance to pivot, to innovate, and to grow. You've shown me that the key to success is not in avoiding failure but in embracing it as a part of the journey. Each failure taught me something new, made me stronger, and brought me closer to my goals.

I learned to view challenges not as roadblocks but as opportunities to learn and evolve. And with each lesson, I became a better entrepreneur, a better leader, and a better person.

Now, as I pen down this letter, I realize that my journey with you, dear Life, has been nothing short of extraordinary. The highs have been exhilarating, and the lows have been humbling. You've taught me to appreciate the beauty in both, to find strength in vulnerability, and to cherish the moments of triumph.

This book is a culmination of all these experiences. It is a tribute to you, dear Life, for being my greatest mentor. Through this book, I want to inspire others to embark on their own entrepreneurial journeys, to dream big, and to never give up. I want to share the stories of the incredible people I've met, the challenges I've overcome, and the lessons I've learned along the way.

As I look back on the past eighteen years, I am filled with gratitude. Gratitude for the opportunities you've given me, the people you've brought into my life, and the lessons you've taught me. You've shaped my path in ways I could never have imagined, and for that, I am eternally grateful. Dear Life, our journey is far from over. There are still many dreams to pursue, many adventures to embark on, and many lessons to learn. As I continue on this path, I carry with me the wisdom and experiences you've bestowed upon me. I am excited to share my story with the world, to inspire others to follow their passions, and to continue building startups that make a difference.

Thank you, dear Life, for being my constant companion, my toughest critic, and my greatest supporter. Here's to the next chapter in our journey—a chapter filled with hope, determination, and endless possibilities.

With all my love and gratitude,
SHARMIN

ABOUT THE TITLE

You may wonder why I decided to title the book as I have. It came to me quite naturally. When my good friend Linda asked me what I was up to one day, I explained that I was writing a book, leading my company, and doing this and doing that, and very soon my friend cut me off: "Bitch, stop! Please . . . " She needed a break just listening to what I was doing, but to me, this is just life. I am a whirlwind, always doing a million things, everywhere, all at once. Maybe that doesn't work for everyone, as burnout is a real thing. But it has certainly been how I have found success. And I would say if that's the response you get from people, you're doing something right.

Now, I hope you enjoy your reading. Start, please . . .

PART 1

EXCITEMENT

CHAPTER 1

THE BIG PITCH

I adjusted my blazer one last time before stepping out of the elevator onto the top floor of one of New York's most prestigious office buildings. I was about to meet Mr. Christopher Brown, a venture capitalist known for his discerning eye and bold investments. This meeting could determine the future of my company. I took a deep breath, reminding myself of the countless hours of preparation I had put in. My company was poised for greatness, and today I was going to secure the investment needed to take it to the next level. "Ms. Ali, Mr. Brown will see you now," said a young assistant, gesturing toward a sleek, glass-walled conference room.

I walked in with confidence, greeted by the sight of Christopher Brown rising from his chair. He extended his hand with a warm smile. "Sharmin, it's a pleasure to finally meet you. Please, have a seat."

"Thank you, Mr. Brown," I replied, taking my seat and setting my portfolio on the table. "I'm thrilled to be here."

"Call me Chris. So, Sharmin, tell me about your company and why you think it's worth a $200 million IPO investment."

I leaned forward, my eyes sparkling with determination. "Chris, my company, Instoried, is at the forefront of developing AI-driven solutions for the marketing industry," I said. "We've created a platform that can gauge emotions in text with 99 percent accuracy and can also provide smart recommendations to increase the emotional engagement that marketers want to strike with

1

their audiences. The potential impact on sales is enormous, and with your investment, I want to make this a global platform."

Chris nodded, intrigued. "That's quite ambitious. What makes your platform stand out from others in the market?"

"Our technology is built on a unique algorithm that we've developed in-house," I explained. "It's more accurate and efficient than anything currently available. We've already seen a 33 percent improvement in marketing performance with our customers. Plus, our team is comprised of experts from both the tech and marketing sectors, giving us a significant advantage."

Chris leaned back in his chair, considering my words. "Impressive. But you must know, going public is a massive undertaking. Why do you want to?"

I smiled, ready for this question. "Timing is everything, Chris. The market is ripe for innovation in AI, especially after the global challenges we've faced recently. Our platform is scalable, and we've laid the groundwork for rapid expansion," I said. "We have interest from major marketing agencies and Fortune 500 companies who are eager to implement our solutions. With your investment, we can accelerate our growth, reach a broader market, and solidify our position as industry leaders."

Chris raised an eyebrow. "And how do you plan to use the $200 million investment?"

I didn't miss a beat. "We'll allocate the funds strategically: 40 percent for R&D to continue improving our technology, 30 percent for market expansion, 20 percent for talent acquisition, and 10 percent for operational costs to ensure a smooth transition to the public market."

Chris nodded, clearly impressed by my thorough plan. "You've done your homework, Sharmin. But let's talk numbers. What kind of returns are you projecting?"

I opened my portfolio and slid a few documents across the table. "Based on our current growth trajectory and market analysis, we're projecting a 20 percent ROI within the first two years post-IPO. Our projections are conservative, considering the potential market size and the increasing demand for AI."

Chris studied the documents, his expression thoughtful. After a few moments, he looked up. "You make a compelling case, Sharmin. But tell me, what drives you? Why are you so passionate about this?"

My gaze softened. "My father is a scientist, and my mother is a lawyer. They have dedicated their lives to helping others and creating an impact, but they often struggled with the inefficiencies in the system. After their retirement, I vowed to create something that would make a real difference," I said. "Entrepreneurship is my way of creating a difference by creating more jobs and impacting millions of lives. This is the only thing I can do."

Chris smiled, clearly moved by my story. "I can see your passion, and I believe in your vision. You've convinced me, Sharmin. I'm willing to commit $200 million to Instoried when you go public."

My heart soared, but I kept my composure. "Thank you, Chris. I promise you won't regret this decision."

Chris extended his hand once more. "I look forward to seeing Instoried change the world." I shook his hand firmly, a triumphant smile spreading across my face.

"Together, we'll make it happen."

As I walked out of the building, I felt a wave of exhilaration. In just thirty minutes, I had secured the investment that would propel my company to new heights. The future was bright, and I was ready to lead Instoried to success.

Securing a $200 million investment from a top venture

capitalist was a pivotal moment in my career. It required confidence, preparation, and, most importantly, being able to cut through the noise with a compelling case for my vision. But as with any entrepreneurial journey, success is often accompanied by unexpected challenges. Just when we were poised for this major breakthrough, unforeseen circumstances led us to take an exit. This experience taught me a valuable lesson about resilience.

CHAPTER 2

THE UNEXPECTED ENCOUNTER

It was early in the morning, and Starbucks in Tribeca was nearly empty. I sat alone in a corner, nursing a lukewarm cup of coffee. Tears streamed down my face as I stared out the window, lost in my thoughts. I was trying to come to terms with the latest heartbreak, feeling more alone than ever in the bustling city. Just as I wiped away another tear, the door chimed, and in walked a woman who looked like she had stepped straight off a runway. She was dressed in luxurious Gucci pajamas and matching slippers, her hair perfectly styled into a messy bun, and her presence exuded confidence and grace. I watched her as she ordered her coffee, wondering who she was and why she looked so familiar.

The woman, with her coffee in hand, scanned the room. Despite the numerous empty tables, she walked straight to my corner. "Hi, do you mind if I join you?" she asked with a warm, knowing smile.

"Do I know you?" I stammered.

"Not yet, but I hope we can change that," she said. "May I?" The woman gestured to the empty seat across from me.

I hesitated but then nodded. "Sure, go ahead."

The woman sat down gracefully and took a sip of her coffee. "I couldn't help but notice you were upset. Want to talk about it?"

I sighed, feeling the weight of my emotions. "It's just . . . I've been having a tough time," I said. "I thought I found the one, but he turned out to be just like the others. It's hard not to feel like I'm the problem."

The woman listened intently, her eyes filled with empathy. "I know how you feel. Believe me, I've been there," she said. "My name is Isa, by the way."

My eyes widened. "Isa? *The* Isa? The billionaire entrepreneur?"

Isa chuckled softly. "Yes, that's me. But today, I'm just a woman who understands heartbreak. Let me tell you a story." I leaned in, intrigued. "Years ago, I was married to a man I thought was my soulmate," she began. "On our wedding night, he slept with his best friend from school. It shattered me when I caught them. I felt humiliated, betrayed, and utterly broken," she continued. "For a while, I lost myself. I couldn't understand how someone I loved so deeply could hurt me so badly."

"That's awful," I said. "How did you get through it?"

Isa took a deep breath. "It wasn't easy. But I realized that I had two choices: let this pain define me, or use it to fuel my growth. I chose the latter. I threw myself into my work, building my startup from the ground up. I focused on my goals, my dreams, and my professional journey. And guess what! My company became a billion-dollar empire." I listened intently, feeling a spark of hope igniting within me. Isa continued, "The men who hurt me, they no longer matter. What matters is the life I've built for myself. I became a professional magnet, attracting opportunities, respect, and yes, even admiration from others. But I never chased anyone. I made myself so powerful and strong that the world came to me." She paused, looking me directly in the eyes. "No matter what happens in your personal life, never lose focus on your professional journey. It is your profession that will create a lasting impact. Make yourself so successful that those who hurt you become insignificant in comparison. The greatest revenge is huge success."

I felt a tear roll down my cheek, but this time it wasn't from sadness. I felt a sense of empowerment I hadn't felt in a long time. "Thank you, Isa. Your words mean more than you know."

Isa smiled. "Anytime, babe. Remember, you have the power to turn your pain into something extraordinary. Now go out there and show the world what you're made of."

As Isa stood to leave, I felt a newfound determination. I watched her walk out the door, and I realized that I, too, could transform my life. I wiped my tears, finished my coffee, and decided it was time to focus on my own journey, one step at a time. With Isa's words echoing in my mind, I stood up, ready to face the world with renewed strength and purpose.

This chance meeting with Isa, a billionaire entrepreneur, became a turning point in my life. Her words of wisdom and encouragement reignited my sense of purpose and determination. Isa's story of turning personal pain into professional success resonated deeply with me and reinforced the importance of nurturing not just my professional aspirations but also my personal well-being and resilience. Isa taught me that by nurturing my inner strength and focusing on my goals, I could overcome any obstacle.

CHAPTER 3

THE CONFIDENCE LESSON

My friend Lily and I were excited to spend our Saturday afternoon at a trendy new restaurant in town. At just seventeen, we felt like grown-ups, venturing into a world of fancy menus and elegant rooftop dining. We pooled our money together and realized we had just enough to share a bowl of soup. As we sat down, Lily and I perused the menu, deciding on a delicious-sounding tomato basil soup. When the waiter came by, we confidently placed the order, feeling proud of our choice. A few minutes later, the waiter returned with a steaming bowl of soup. We were thrilled, but as the waiter walked away, Lily checked her wallet, and her face turned pale. "Sharmin, we don't have enough money to pay for this," she whispered urgently.

I felt a rush of panic, but then an idea struck me. I glanced around and noticed a few mosquitoes buzzing nearby. "Lily, I've got an idea," I said, my voice steady. "Trust me on this." I carefully caught one of the mosquitoes, swatted it, and discreetly placed it into the soup. Taking a deep breath, I called the waiter over. "Excuse me, sir," I said, trying to sound as calm and confident as possible. "There's a mosquito in our soup."

The waiter looked horrified. "Oh, my goodness! I am so sorry. Let me get the manager."

A moment later, the manager appeared, his face a mix of

concern and embarrassment. "I am terribly sorry about this," he said. "This is unacceptable. Please, allow us to bring you a new bowl of soup, on the house."

I shook my head, my expression firm. "No, thank you. We're quite disappointed, and honestly, we're not hungry anymore. We'd prefer to leave."

The manager nodded, eager to avoid further trouble. "Of course, there's no need to pay. We apologize for this inconvenience."

Lily and I stood up, and as we walked out of the restaurant, my heart was pounding. Once we were a safe distance away, Lily turned to me, eyes wide with admiration. "Sharmin, that was incredible! How did you come up with that so fast?"

I shrugged, a smile tugging at my lips. "I just thought on my feet," I said. "I realized we needed to avoid embarrassment, so I came up with a plan. I guess sometimes confidence means staying calm and finding a solution, no matter how tricky the situation is."

Lily nodded, clearly impressed. "You know, Sharmin, you have a knack for thinking on your feet. It's like you can handle anything."

As we walked away, I felt a newfound sense of confidence as a seventeen-year-old. I realized that I had the ability to come up with spontaneous ideas and navigate tricky situations. That day at the restaurant taught me an invaluable lesson: confidence isn't just about being sure of yourself; it's about staying composed and resourceful, even when things don't go as planned. From that moment on, I carried that confidence with me, knowing I could tackle whatever challenges came my way.

Placing a mosquito in our soup and convincing the manager to let us leave without paying was a bold move that demonstrated the power of being adaptable and thinking on your feet. This experience instilled in me a sense of confidence that has been invaluable in my entrepreneurial journey. Confidence and adaptability are crucial, but so is having a clear vision and passion for what you do.

CHAPTER 4

LUNA

One summer morning in India, at the tender age of seven, I was out for a brisk morning walk, my breath visible in the crisp air of the quiet neighborhood. The streets were empty, making my solitary walk feel even more serene. I enjoyed these moments of solitude, finding solace in the rhythm of my steps and the fresh morning air.

As I rounded a corner, I spotted a familiar sight: a stray dog, Luna, that I had often fed on my walks. Luna, with its patchy fur and soulful eyes, had become a comforting presence over the past months. I smiled, expecting the usual friendly greeting. But today, something was different. Without warning, Luna lunged at me, teeth bared, and bit my leg. Pain shot through me, and I stumbled back, crying out in surprise and agony. Luna, looking just as startled as me, backed away and fled down the street.

I clutched my leg, tears streaming down my face. I managed to limp to a nearby bench and call for help. Soon, a neighbor arrived and rushed me to the doctor. The pain was intense, and I felt a mix of confusion and hurt. Why had Luna, whom I had cared for, attacked me?

At the doctor's clinic, I was given a series of injections to prevent infection. Each prick of the needle was a stark reminder of the unexpected betrayal I felt. As I sat there, the events replayed in my mind. Why had Luna bitten me?

The next day, with my leg bandaged and my steps cautious,

I decided to find out more about what had happened. I spoke to some neighbors and soon learned the unfortunate truth: someone had beaten Luna the previous evening. The poor animal had been terrified and traumatized.

Understanding dawned on me. Luna had bitten me out of fear, not malice. The dog had been scared, just trying to protect itself in a world that had suddenly become threatening. My heart ached for the poor creature.

That afternoon as I sat on my porch, Luna approached me cautiously, then lay down beside me, eyes full of remorse and sorrow. I reached out a hand, my fingers gently brushing Luna's fur. In that moment, I felt a deep connection with the dog. Luna was trying to apologize, to show that it had not meant to harm me.

I realized the lesson the dog was teaching me. Empathy isn't just about understanding others' pain but also recognizing the circumstances that lead to their actions. The dog had been scared, hurt, and defensive, just as any creature would be in such a situation.

From that day on, my walks were different. As a seven-year-old, I walked with a deeper understanding of the world around me, seeing the pain and fear that often lay beneath the surface. And each morning, Luna would join me, a silent companion who had taught me the true meaning of empathy.

CHAPTER 5
THE ELIXIR OF ASCENDANCE

I had always dreamt of embarking on a journey that would challenge me physically and spiritually. So, when the opportunity arose to trek the Camino Inca from Cusco to Machu Picchu, I seized it with fervor. The promise of adventure and self-discovery on this five-day trek was a beacon in my life.

Armed with a backpack, sturdy boots, and a heart full of determination, I joined a small group of trekkers. We were led by a local guide who knew every twist and turn of the Inca Trail. The path was arduous, winding through dense forests, steep inclines, and narrow passes. Each day brought new challenges and dangers: treacherous cliff edges, unpredictable weather, and the sheer physical exhaustion that came from hiking at high altitudes. Despite the difficulties, I found solace in the breathtaking scenery. The Andes Mountains loomed majestically around me, their peaks touching the heavens. The air was thin but crisp, filled with the scent of wildflowers and the distant sounds of exotic birds. The camaraderie among the trekkers also kept my spirits high; they shared stories, laughter, and encouragement during the toughest parts of the journey.

On the third day, as we camped near the ruins of an ancient Incan village, a shamanic healer visited our camp. She was a mysterious-looking figure, about ninety years old, dressed in an ankle-length skirt with a braided waistband. She wore a cap on her head, and pinned to her hair was a folded piece of cloth. Her piercing eyes seemed to see into the very soul, and she spoke of the transformative powers of ayahuasca, a sacred brew used for centuries by the Indigenous people of the Amazon for spiritual enlightenment and healing. Intrigued and seeking deeper meaning in my life, I agreed to participate in an ayahuasca ceremony that night.

As the shaman chanted ancient prayers and the brew took effect, I felt myself slipping into a trance. Colors and shapes danced before my eyes, and I felt a profound connection to the earth and the cosmos. Visions of my past, my struggles, and my fears swirled around me, but they seemed distant and unimportant. I felt a surge of clarity and peace, as if the burdens I had carried for so long were being lifted from my shoulders. The next morning, renewed and filled with a sense of purpose, I continued the trek.

On the fifth and final day, I reached the Sun Gate, the entrance to the majestic Machu Picchu. The ancient city lay before me, shrouded in mist and mystery. We made our way to the summit of the mountain, where I stood at the edge, looking down at the awe-inspiring landscape below. It was there, at the pinnacle of my journey, that I had my most profound experience. I felt the presence of the mountain as if it were a living, breathing entity. I spoke aloud, pouring out my heart, my fears, and my doubts. I asked for guidance, for a sign that I was on the right path.

In the silence that followed, I felt a deep, resonant voice within myself. It was the mountain speaking, its wisdom echoing in my mind. "Sharmin," it said, "your challenges are the stones that pave your path. Embrace them, for they will lead you to your destiny. Focus not on the obstacles but on the vast horizon before you. Let your goals be as towering as these peaks, and every problem will seem but a pebble in comparison." Tears streamed down my face as the realization dawned on me. I had been consumed by my fears and insecurities, allowing them to overshadow my true potential. But now, I saw clearly. My life's purpose was immense, and I was capable of achieving greatness. With newfound resolve, I descended the mountain. The trek back was swift, my steps were lighter, my heart was filled with a sense of mission. I knew that my life's challenges were not barriers but stepping stones to something greater. The wisdom of Machu Picchu had illuminated my path, giving me the clarity and inspiration to pursue my dreams with unwavering determination.

The moral of this journey was clear: Make your life goals so significant and tremendous that every other problem seems insignificant in front of them. With the mountain's guidance and the elixir of ascendance coursing through my veins, I was ready to embrace my destiny and achieve greatness beyond my wildest dreams.

PART II

PLATEAU

CHAPTER 6

THE RELATIONSHIP QUADRANT

THE FIRST QUADRANT: THE IMPACT OF POOR PARENTING ON CHILDREN'S LIVES AND FUTURE

Parenting is one of the most significant responsibilities an individual can undertake, shaping the emotional, psychological, and social development of a child. Poor parenting can have far-reaching and often devastating effects on a child's life, influencing their behavior, mental health, and future relationships. Understanding the various factors that contribute to poor parenting and the subsequent impact on children is crucial for fostering healthier family dynamics and promoting the well-being of future generations.

Factors Affecting a Child's Life Due to Poor Parenting

🟐 EMOTIONAL AND PSYCHOLOGICAL DEVELOPMENT

Poor parenting can severely impact a child's emotional and psychological development. Children who do not receive adequate emotional support, affection, and validation from their parents often struggle with low self-esteem, anxiety, and depression. These children may grow up feeling unloved, unworthy, and constantly seeking approval from others, which can lead to a host of mental health issues.

EXAMPLE A child who is consistently criticized or belittled by their parents may develop an inferiority complex, leading to chronic low self-esteem and social anxiety. This can affect their academic performance, peer relationships, and overall sense of well-being.

2 BEHAVIORAL ISSUES

Children exposed to poor parenting are more likely to exhibit behavioral problems, including aggression, defiance, and antisocial behavior. Lack of proper guidance, discipline, and positive reinforcement can result in children struggling to understand boundaries, respect authority, and develop self-control.

EXAMPLE A child raised in a chaotic and inconsistent environment may have difficulty following rules and understanding the consequences of their actions. This can lead to frequent conflicts at school and in social settings, making it challenging for them to form healthy relationships.

3 ACADEMIC PERFORMANCE

The quality of parenting has a direct impact on a child's academic performance. Children who do not receive adequate support and encouragement from their parents may struggle with motivation, concentration, and confidence in their academic abilities. Poor parenting can also result in a lack of structure and routine, further hindering a child's ability to succeed in school.

EXAMPLE A child who does not receive help with homework

or encouragement to pursue their interests may fall behind academically, leading to poor grades and limited opportunities for higher education and career advancement.

❹ SOCIAL SKILLS AND RELATIONSHIPS

Children learn social skills and how to form relationships primarily from their parents. Poor parenting can result in children having difficulty developing healthy interpersonal skills, leading to issues with forming and maintaining friendships, romantic relationships, and professional connections.

EXAMPLE A child who witnesses constant conflict or neglect within the family may struggle with trust and communication in their relationships, making it challenging to establish meaningful connections with others.

Reasons Why Parents Fail to Bring Up Kids in a Healthy Way

❶ LACK OF PARENTING SKILLS

Many parents lack the necessary skills and knowledge to raise children effectively. This can be due to a lack of education, experience, or exposure to positive parenting models. Without proper guidance, parents may resort to ineffective or harmful parenting practices.

EXAMPLE Parents who were raised in abusive or neglectful environments themselves may not know how to provide the emotional support and structure their children need, perpetuating a cycle of poor parenting.

❷ ECONOMIC STRESS

Financial difficulties can place immense stress on parents, affecting their ability to provide for their children's basic needs and emotional well-being. Economic stress can lead to parents working long hours, struggling to make ends meet, and experiencing elevated levels of anxiety and frustration, which can negatively impact their parenting.

EXAMPLE: A parent working multiple jobs to support the family may have limited time and energy to spend with their children, leading to feelings of neglect and abandonment.

❸ MENTAL HEALTH ISSUES

Parents dealing with mental health issues such as depression, anxiety, or substance abuse may find it challenging to provide a stable and nurturing environment for their children. These issues can impair a parent's ability to engage with their children, manage stress, and maintain consistent parenting practices.

EXAMPLE: A parent suffering from severe depression may struggle to get out of bed, let alone attend to their child's emotional and physical needs, leading to a lack of supervision and support.

❹ RELATIONSHIP PROBLEMS

Conflict and instability within a marriage or partnership can create a toxic environment for children. Parents who are constantly arguing, separated, or divorced may inadvertently expose their children to emotional turmoil and insecurity, affecting their sense of stability and safety.

EXAMPLE: A child caught in the middle of parental conflict may experience confusion, fear, and guilt, leading to emotional and behavioral problems.

✿ LACK OF SUPPORT SYSTEMS

Raising children without a strong support system can be overwhelming for parents. The absence of extended family, friends, or community resources can leave parents feeling isolated and unsupported, making it difficult to cope with the challenges of parenting.

EXAMPLE A single parent without access to childcare or support from family and friends may struggle to balance work and parenting responsibilities, leading to stress and burnout.

Factors Leading to Child Depression Due to Poor Parenting

➊ EMOTIONAL NEGLECT

Emotional neglect occurs when parents fail to provide the necessary emotional support, attention, and affection that children need to feel valued and secure. This can lead to feelings of loneliness, worthlessness, and depression in children.

EXAMPLE A child who feels ignored or dismissed by their parents may internalize these feelings, leading to chronic sadness and a lack of self-worth.

➋ INCONSISTENT PARENTING

Inconsistent parenting, characterized by unpredictable and erratic behavior from parents, can create confusion and insecurity in children. When children do not know what to expect from their parents, they may develop anxiety and depressive symptoms.

EXAMPLE A parent who alternates between being overly strict and permissive may leave a child feeling uncertain and fearful about how to behave, leading to emotional distress.

❸ PARENTAL CRITICISM AND REJECTION

Constant criticism and rejection from parents can damage a child's self-esteem and lead to feelings of inadequacy and depression. Children who are made to feel that they can never meet their parents' expectations may struggle with chronic self-doubt and sadness.

EXAMPLE A child who is consistently told they are not good enough or that their efforts are worthless may develop a persistent sense of failure and hopelessness.

❹ EXPOSURE TO DOMESTIC VIOLENCE

Witnessing or experiencing domestic violence can have severe psychological effects on children. The trauma and fear associated with domestic violence can lead to anxiety, depression, and post-traumatic stress disorder (PTSD).

EXAMPLE A child who sees one parent physically or verbally abuse the other may feel scared, helpless, and guilty, leading to long-term emotional scars.

LONG-TERM IMPACT OF POOR PARENTING ON CHILDREN'S FUTURES

❶ MENTAL HEALTH ISSUES

Children raised in environments characterized by poor parenting are at a higher risk of developing mental health issues such as depression, anxiety, and PTSD. These issues can persist into adulthood, affecting their overall quality of life.

EXAMPLE An adult who experienced neglect and abuse as a child may struggle with chronic depression and anxiety, impacting their ability to maintain employment and relationships.

❷ DIFFICULTY IN RELATIONSHIPS

Poor parenting can lead to difficulties in forming and maintaining healthy relationships. Children who do not learn appropriate social skills and emotional regulation may struggle with trust, communication, and intimacy in their relationships.

EXAMPLE An individual who grew up in a dysfunctional family may find it challenging to form close bonds with others, leading to feelings of isolation and loneliness.

❸ ACADEMIC AND CAREER CHALLENGES

The lack of support and encouragement from parents can hinder a child's academic performance and career prospects. Children who do not receive the necessary guidance and resources may struggle to achieve their full potential.

EXAMPLE A young adult who did not receive academic support from their parents may have limited career opportunities and face difficulties in achieving financial stability.

❹ INCREASED RISK OF SUBSTANCE ABUSE

Children from unstable and neglectful homes are at a higher risk of turning to substance abuse as a coping mechanism. The absence of healthy coping strategies and emotional support can lead to experimentation with drugs and alcohol.

EXAMPLE A teenager who feels neglected and unsupported by their parents may turn to alcohol or drugs to escape their emotional pain, leading to addiction and further complications.

🌸 PERPETUATION OF POOR PARENTING

Unfortunately, the cycle of poor parenting can perpetuate itself. Children who grow up in dysfunctional environments may lack positive parenting models and may replicate these behaviors with their own children.

EXAMPLE An adult who experienced abuse and neglect as a child may struggle to provide a nurturing and stable environment for their own children, continuing the cycle of poor parenting.

The impact of poor parenting on children's lives and futures is profound and multifaceted. Emotional and psychological development, behavioral issues, academic performance, social skills, and mental health are all areas that can be significantly affected by poor parenting practices. Understanding the reasons behind poor parenting, such as lack of skills, economic stress, mental health issues, relationship problems, and lack of support systems, is crucial for addressing and mitigating these negative effects.

Parents play a vital role in shaping their children's future, and the consequences of poor parenting can last a lifetime. It is essential for parents to seek help and resources to improve their parenting skills and create a supportive and nurturing environment for their children. By addressing the underlying factors that contribute to poor parenting, and implementing positive parenting practices, we can break the cycle of dysfunction and promote healthier, happier futures for our children.

THE SECOND QUADRANT: THE POWER OF FRIENDSHIP— HOW FRIENDS SHAPE OUR LIVES

Friendship is a fundamental aspect of human experience, playing a crucial role in shaping our lives. The people we choose to surround ourselves with can significantly influence our mental, emotional, and even physical well-being. Good friends provide support, encouragement, and companionship, while negative friendships can lead to detrimental effects. This section explores the profound impact friends can have on our lives, illustrating with various stories how friendships can either elevate us to new heights or drag us down.

The Positive Impact of Good Friends

❶ EMOTIONAL SUPPORT AND ENCOURAGEMENT

Good friends are a source of emotional support and encouragement. They stand by us in times of need, offering comfort and advice that can help us navigate life's challenges.

EXAMPLE Sarah and Emily had been best friends since childhood. When Sarah's mother passed away unexpectedly, she was devastated. Emily, who had always been a pillar of support, stayed by Sarah's side throughout the grieving process. She listened to Sarah's feelings, shared her own experiences of loss, and helped Sarah find a grief counselor. Emily's unwavering support gave Sarah the strength to cope with her loss and gradually rebuild her life. This experience deepened their bond and highlighted the importance of having a friend who can offer genuine emotional support.

🟌 MOTIVATION AND INSPIRATION

Friends can motivate and inspire us to pursue our goals and dreams. They can push us out of our comfort zones and encourage us to strive for excellence.

EXAMPLE Mark had always dreamed of running a marathon, but he lacked the confidence and discipline to train consistently. His friend James, an avid runner, encouraged him to start training and even offered to run with him. James's enthusiasm and dedication inspired Mark to commit to a rigorous training schedule. Over months of preparation, James's constant encouragement kept Mark motivated. Eventually, Mark completed his first marathon, a feat he would never have achieved without James's support and inspiration.

🟌 PROVIDING A SENSE OF BELONGING

Having friends gives us a sense of belonging and community. Friends can create an environment where we feel accepted and valued for who we are.

EXAMPLE Rachel moved to a new city for her job and felt incredibly lonely. She missed her family and friends back home. One day, she decided to join a local art club, hoping to meet new people. There, she met a group of friendly and welcoming individuals who shared her passion for painting. Over time, Rachel formed close bonds with her fellow club members, who became her new friends. They supported her creative pursuits, celebrated her successes, and were there for her during difficult times. The art club became a place where Rachel felt a strong sense of belonging and community.

❹ PROMOTING HEALTHY LIFESTYLES

Good friends can encourage us to adopt healthier lifestyles. Whether it's through exercising together, eating well, or avoiding harmful habits, friends can play a significant role in our physical well-being.

EXAMPLE Linda and Karen had been friends since college. After graduation, Linda started gaining weight due to a sedentary lifestyle and poor eating habits. Concerned about her health, Karen suggested they join a gym together. They started working out regularly and cooking healthy meals at home. Karen's companionship and support made the lifestyle change enjoyable for Linda. Over time, Linda lost weight, felt more energetic, and developed a healthier relationship with food and exercise. Karen's influence helped Linda transform her health and well-being.

The Negative Impact of Toxic Friends

❶ ENCOURAGING HARMFUL BEHAVIOR

Toxic friends can influence us to engage in harmful behavior, leading to negative consequences for our health and well-being.

EXAMPLE Alex was a responsible and focused student, but his new friend, Tom, was a party enthusiast who frequently indulged in excessive drinking and reckless behavior. Wanting to fit in, Alex started joining Tom at parties and adopted his habits. Soon, Alex's grades began to slip, and he found himself in trouble with the law due to a DUI incident. Tom's influence led Alex down a path of self-destruction, highlighting how toxic friendships can encourage harmful behavior.

❷ UNDERMINING SELF-ESTEEM

Negative friends can undermine our self-esteem and confidence through constant criticism, manipulation, or jealousy.

EXAMPLE Jessica was excited about her promotion at work, but her friend Megan's reaction was far from supportive. Instead of congratulating her, Megan made snide comments about how Jessica must have gotten the promotion through favoritism. Over time, Megan's constant negativity and backhanded compliments chipped away at Jessica's confidence. Jessica began doubting her abilities and felt undeserving of her achievements. Megan's toxic behavior demonstrated how negative friends can undermine one's self-esteem and emotional well-being.

❸ CREATING EMOTIONAL STRESS

Toxic friendships can be a significant source of emotional stress, leading to anxiety, depression, and other mental health issues.

EXAMPLE Michael had been friends with Ethan since high school, but as they grew older, Ethan's behavior became increasingly erratic and demanding. Ethan would frequently call Michael in the middle of the night, expecting immediate attention and help with his problems. When Michael couldn't always be available, Ethan would guilt-trip him and make him feel like a bad friend. The constant emotional stress took a toll on Michael's mental health, leading to anxiety and depression. Ethan's toxic behavior highlighted how emotionally draining negative friendships could be.

The Importance of Choosing Good Friends

Given the significant impact friends can have on our lives, it is crucial to choose friends who positively influence our well-being and personal growth. Surrounding ourselves with good friends can lead to a happier, healthier, and more fulfilling life.

❶ BUILDING A SUPPORTIVE NETWORK

Having a supportive network of friends can provide a safety net during challenging times. These friends offer advice, share their experiences, and help us navigate difficult situations.

EXAMPLE: Laura was diagnosed with breast cancer, and the news was devastating. However, her friends rallied around her, providing unwavering support throughout her treatment. They accompanied her to appointments, organized fundraisers to help with medical expenses, and stayed by her side during chemotherapy sessions. Laura's friends' support gave her the strength to fight the disease and maintain a positive outlook. Their collective efforts demonstrated the importance of having a strong and supportive network of friends.

❷ ENHANCING PERSONAL GROWTH

Good friends encourage us to grow and develop as individuals. They challenge us to step out of our comfort zones and pursue our passions and interests.

EXAMPLE: David had always been interested in photography but never pursued it seriously. His friends, recognizing his talent, encouraged him to take photography classes and even gifted him a professional camera. With their encouragement, David honed his skills and eventually started his own photography business. His friends' belief in his potential pushed him to follow his passion, leading to personal and professional growth.

✿ PROVIDING HONEST FEEDBACK

Good friends provide honest feedback that helps us improve and make better decisions. They offer constructive criticism with our best interests at heart.

EXAMPLE Emma was considering a career change but was unsure if it was the right move. She confided in her friend Olivia, who listened attentively and then provided honest feedback. Olivia pointed out Emma's strengths and areas for improvement, helping her evaluate the decision objectively. With Olivia's insightful advice, Emma made an informed choice that led to greater career satisfaction. Olivia's honest feedback exemplified how good friends could provide valuable guidance.

✿ CREATING LASTING MEMORIES

Friendships enrich our lives with shared experiences and lasting memories. These moments of joy, laughter, and adventure create bonds that withstand the test of time.

EXAMPLE Chris and his group of friends loved adventure. They planned regular hiking trips, camping excursions, and travel adventures. These experiences not only brought them closer together but also created a treasure trove of memories that they cherished. The camaraderie and joy they shared during these adventures highlighted how friendships could create lasting memories that enrich our lives.

Friends play a vital role in shaping our lives—influencing our emotional, mental, and physical well-being. Good friends provide support, encouragement, and companionship, helping us navigate life's challenges and celebrate its joys. On the other hand, toxic friendships can lead to negative consequences, including harmful behavior, poor self-esteem, and emotional stress.

Choosing good friends who positively influence our lives is crucial for our overall well-being and personal growth. By surrounding ourselves with supportive, inspiring, and honest friends, we can build a strong network that helps us thrive. The stories of Sarah and Emily, Mark and James, Rachel and the art club, Linda and Karen, Alex and Tom, Jessica and Megan, Michael and Ethan, Laura and her supportive network, David and his growth-oriented friends, and Emma and Olivia illustrate the profound impact friends can have on our lives. Ultimately, the power of friendship lies in its ability to uplift, inspire, and support us through life's journey. Investing in good friendships and nurturing these relationships can lead to a happier, healthier, and more fulfilling life.

THE THIRD QUADRANT: THE IMPACT OF A HEALTHY PARTNER ON PERSONAL GROWTH

Relationships are foundational to human experience—influencing our happiness, health, and personal development. A healthy relationship with a partner can be a source of immense support, motivation, and growth. Conversely, unhealthy relationships can hinder personal progress and contribute to emotional turmoil. Here, we'll explore the significant role a healthy partner can play in our lives, illustrating through various examples how positive relationships can lead to personal growth and fulfillment.

Healthy relationships are characterized by mutual respect, trust, support, and open communication. These elements create a nurturing environment where both partners can thrive and grow. A healthy partner encourages personal development, provides emotional support, and helps navigate life's challenges, making the journey more fulfilling and rewarding.

Personal Growth through Emotional Support

❶ PROVIDING UNWAVERING SUPPORT

A healthy partner stands by us through thick and thin, offering unwavering support during challenging times. This emotional backing can significantly enhance our resilience and ability to cope with stress.

EXAMPLE: Emma and John had been married for five years when Emma decided to pursue a master's degree while working full-time. The decision was daunting, and she often felt overwhelmed by the demands of her job and studies. John, recognizing the importance of her educational goals, took on extra household responsibilities, and provided constant encouragement. He listened to her frustrations and celebrated her small victories. John's unwavering support helped Emma stay focused and motivated, leading to her successfully completing her degree. This experience not only strengthened their relationship but also demonstrated the importance of having a supportive partner.

❷ ENCOURAGING SELF-CONFIDENCE

A healthy partner believes in our abilities and encourages us to pursue our passions, boosting our self-confidence and helping us achieve our goals.

EXAMPLE: Rachel had always dreamed of starting her own bakery, but she was plagued by self-doubt. Her boyfriend, Lucas, saw her potential and encouraged her to take the leap. He helped her draft a business plan and find a suitable location, and even assisted with marketing strategies. Whenever Rachel doubted herself, Lucas reminded her of her talent and dedication. His belief in her abilities gave Rachel the confidence to open her bakery, which soon became a local favorite. Lucas's encouragement played a crucial role in helping Rachel realize her dream and build a successful business.

Personal Growth through Mutual Inspiration

1 FOSTERING PERSONAL DEVELOPMENT

Healthy partners inspire each other to grow and improve. They support each other's goals and aspirations, creating an environment where personal development is encouraged and celebrated.

EXAMPLE Mike and Sarah were both passionate about personal development. They frequently discussed their goals and dreams, pushing each other to strive for excellence. Mike encouraged Sarah to take a leadership course that would help her advance in her career, while Sarah motivated Mike to complete his novel. Their mutual support and inspiration led to significant personal growth for both of them. Sarah earned a promotion at work, and Mike finished his book, which was eventually published. Their relationship thrived on the shared commitment to personal development.

2 CREATING A HEALTHY LIFESTYLE

A healthy partner can motivate us to adopt healthier habits, leading to improved physical and mental well-being. Shared activities such as exercising, cooking nutritious meals, or practicing mindfulness can enhance our quality of life.

EXAMPLE Alex and Mia decided to embark on a health journey together. They started by incorporating regular exercise into their routine, joining a local gym, and attending fitness classes. They also began experimenting with healthy recipes, transforming their diet. The positive changes in their lifestyle improved their physical health and brought them closer as a couple. They felt more energetic, happier, and more connected. Alex and Mia's commitment to a healthy lifestyle demonstrated how partners could inspire and support each other in making positive changes.

Personal Growth through Effective Communication

❶ RESOLVING CONFLICTS CONSTRUCTIVELY

Healthy relationships are built on effective communication and the ability to resolve conflicts constructively. A partner who communicates openly and respectfully helps us navigate disagreements and find mutually beneficial solutions.

EXAMPLE: Jessica and Tom had a strong relationship, but like all couples, they faced conflicts. Instead of letting disagreements fester, they practiced open and honest communication. They set aside time to discuss their issues calmly, focusing on finding solutions rather than blaming each other. This approach helped them resolve conflicts quickly and strengthened their bond. Their ability to communicate effectively ensured that their relationship remained healthy and supportive, even during challenging times.

❷ PROMOTING EMOTIONAL INTELLIGENCE

A healthy partner helps us develop emotional intelligence by encouraging self-awareness, empathy, and understanding. This growth can enhance our relationships with others and improve our overall emotional well-being.

EXAMPLE: Daniel struggled with expressing his emotions, often bottling up his feelings. His girlfriend, Olivia, noticed this and gently encouraged him to open up. She practiced active listening, creating a safe space for Daniel to share his thoughts and feelings. Over time, Daniel became more comfortable with emotional expression and developed greater empathy and understanding. Olivia's support helped him grow emotionally, strengthening their relationship and improving his interactions with others.

Personal Growth through Shared Goals and Dreams

❶ ACHIEVING SHARED DREAMS

Having a partner who shares our goals and dreams can be incredibly motivating. Working together toward common objectives fosters a sense of unity and purpose, enhancing personal growth and relationship satisfaction.

EXAMPLE: Sophie and Liam dreamed of traveling the world together. They set a goal to save money and plan an extended trip across several continents. Working toward this shared dream, they budgeted carefully, researched destinations, and learned about different cultures. The journey brought them closer, and the experiences they shared deepened their bond. Achieving their shared dream was a testament to their teamwork and commitment, highlighting the positive impact of pursuing common goals with a partner.

❷ SUPPORTING CAREER ASPIRATIONS

A healthy partner supports our career aspirations, providing encouragement and practical assistance. This support can lead to significant professional growth and fulfillment.

EXAMPLE Ethan had always aspired to start his own tech company, but the risks and uncertainties held him back. Grace, his wife, believed in his vision and encouraged him to take the plunge. She helped him secure funding, provided valuable feedback on his business plan, and managed household responsibilities to give Ethan the time he needed to focus on his startup. With Grace's support, Ethan's company flourished, and he achieved his entrepreneurial dream. Grace's belief in Ethan and her practical assistance were crucial to his professional success.

The Negative Impact of Unhealthy Relationships

While healthy relationships foster personal growth, unhealthy relationships can have the opposite effect, leading to emotional distress, decreased self-esteem, and stunted personal development.

① UNDERMINING SELF-WORTH

Unhealthy partners can undermine our self-worth through criticism, manipulation, or lack of support. This behavior can erode our confidence and hinder our ability to achieve our goals.

EXAMPLE Rachel was in a relationship with Matt, who frequently belittled her achievements and criticized her choices. His constant negativity made Rachel doubt herself and feel inadequate. She lost confidence in her abilities and became hesitant to pursue her dreams. Matt's toxic behavior highlighted how an unhealthy partner could undermine self-worth and hinder personal growth.

② CREATING EMOTIONAL TURMOIL

Unhealthy relationships can be a significant source of emotional turmoil, leading to anxiety, depression, and other mental health issues. The constant stress and conflict can negatively impact our overall well-being.

EXAMPLE Laura was in a tumultuous relationship with Steve, who was controlling and prone to outbursts of anger. The constant emotional stress took a toll on Laura's mental health, leading to anxiety and depression. She felt trapped and powerless, unable to focus on her personal and professional goals. Steve's behavior illustrated the damaging effects of an unhealthy relationship on emotional well-being.

A healthy partner plays a crucial role in our personal growth and overall well-being. They provide emotional support, encouragement, and inspiration, helping us navigate life's challenges and achieve our goals. Through effective communication, shared goals, and mutual respect, healthy relationships create an environment where both partners can thrive.

The stories above demonstrate the profound impact a healthy partner can have on our lives. These examples highlight the importance of nurturing and maintaining positive relationships that foster personal growth and fulfillment. Conversely, unhealthy relationships can undermine self-worth, create emotional turmoil, and hinder personal development. The stories of Rachel and Matt and Laura and Steve serve as cautionary tales about the negative impact of toxic relationships. Ultimately, the power of a healthy relationship lies in its ability to support, inspire, and uplift us. Investing in healthy partnerships and nurturing these relationships can lead to a happier, healthier, and more fulfilling life.

THE FOURTH QUADRANT: THE IMPORTANCE OF A HEALTHY RELATIONSHIP WITH WORK

In today's fast-paced world, work is an integral part of our lives. It provides financial stability, a sense of purpose, and an avenue for personal and professional growth. However, an unhealthy relationship with work can lead to significant mental, emotional, and physical stress. Striking a balance between work and personal life is crucial to maintaining overall well-being. This section explores why it is essential to have a healthy relationship with work; the negative impacts of a stressful work life; and strategies to achieve a balanced, fulfilling work experience.

The Significance of a Healthy Work-Life Relationship

A healthy relationship with work means finding a balance that allows us to perform our job effectively while also maintaining our mental, emotional, and physical health. This balance ensures that work remains a source of satisfaction and growth rather than stress and burnout.

❶ MENTAL AND EMOTIONAL WELL-BEING

A healthy work–life balance is critical for maintaining mental and emotional well-being. When work demands become overwhelming, they can lead to chronic stress, anxiety, and depression. Conversely, a balanced approach to work can foster a sense of accomplishment and satisfaction.

❷ PHYSICAL HEALTH

Excessive work stress can take a toll on physical health, leading to issues such as high blood pressure, heart disease, and weakened immune function. A balanced work life promotes better physical health through adequate rest, exercise, and a healthy lifestyle.

✿ PERSONAL RELATIONSHIPS

Maintaining a healthy work–life balance allows us to nurture personal relationships with family and friends. It ensures we have time and energy to invest in these connections, which are vital for our emotional support and overall happiness.

✿ JOB SATISFACTION AND PERFORMANCE

A balanced work life can enhance job satisfaction and performance. When we manage our workload effectively, we are more productive, creative, and motivated. This leads to better job performance and a more fulfilling career.

The Negative Impact of a Stressful Work Life

A stressful relationship with work can have far-reaching consequences, affecting various aspects of our lives. Understanding these impacts can help us recognize the importance of balancing work and personal life.

✿ CHRONIC STRESS AND BURNOUT

Chronic stress is one of the most common outcomes of an unhealthy work life. When job demands consistently exceed our capacity to cope, it can lead to burnout, characterized by physical and emotional exhaustion, cynicism, and decreased productivity.

EXAMPLE Sarah, a marketing executive, was known for her dedication and hard work. However, as her company grew, so did her responsibilities. She found herself working long hours, often sacrificing weekends and holidays. Over time, Sarah began experiencing severe fatigue, anxiety, and a loss of interest in her work. She eventually reached a point of burnout, where even the simplest tasks felt overwhelming. Sarah's experience highlighted the detrimental effects of chronic stress and the importance of maintaining a healthy work–life balance.

❷ IMPACT ON MENTAL HEALTH

A stressful work environment can contribute to mental health issues such as anxiety and depression. The constant pressure to perform, meet deadlines, and achieve targets can create a sense of helplessness and low self-esteem.

EXAMPLE Tom, a software developer, worked in a highly competitive industry. His company set unrealistic deadlines, leading to constant pressure and long hours. Tom began experiencing severe anxiety, characterized by panic attacks and insomnia. The relentless stress affected his mental health, making it difficult for him to concentrate and perform at his best. Tom's situation underscored the need for a balanced work life to maintain mental health.

❸ STRAINED PERSONAL RELATIONSHIPS

Work-related stress can spill over into our personal lives, straining relationships with family and friends. When work demands dominate our time and energy, it leaves little room for nurturing these important connections.

EXAMPLE Lisa, a project manager, was passionate about her job. However, her demanding schedule left her with little time for her family. She often missed family events and spent weekends catching up on work. Over time, her relationships with her spouse and children became strained, leading to feelings of guilt and isolation. Lisa's experience highlighted how an imbalanced work life could negatively impact personal relationships.

4 DECREASED PRODUCTIVITY AND JOB SATISFACTION

Ironically, excessive work stress can lead to decreased productivity and job satisfaction. When we are overwhelmed and exhausted, our focus and effective performance diminish, leading to lower job satisfaction and motivation.

EXAMPLE Mark, a financial analyst, prided himself on his work ethic. However, the constant pressure to meet tight deadlines led to severe stress and exhaustion. As a result, Mark's productivity declined, and he began making mistakes in his work. His job satisfaction plummeted, and he started questioning his career choices. Mark's situation demonstrated how a stressful work life could lead to decreased productivity and job satisfaction.

Strategies for Achieving a Healthy Work-Life Balance

Achieving a healthy work–life balance requires intentional effort and effective strategies. Here are several ways to ensure that our passion for work doesn't turn into the biggest pain in our lives.

1 SET BOUNDARIES

Setting clear boundaries between work and personal life is crucial. This means defining specific work hours and sticking to them, avoiding work-related tasks during personal time, and communicating these boundaries to colleagues and supervisors.

EXAMPLE Emma, a graphic designer, realized that her work was encroaching on her personal life. She decided to set clear boundaries by establishing specific work hours and avoiding work-related activities after those hours. Emma also communicated these boundaries to her clients and colleagues, ensuring they respected her personal time. This strategy helped Emma regain control over her work–life balance and improve her overall well-being.

❷ PRIORITIZE SELF-CARE

Prioritizing self-care is essential for maintaining a healthy work–life balance. This includes regular exercise, a balanced diet, adequate sleep, and engaging in activities that bring joy and relaxation.

EXAMPLE: Tom, the software developer who struggled with anxiety, decided to prioritize self-care. He started practicing mindfulness meditation, exercising regularly, and ensuring he got enough sleep. Tom also made time for hobbies such as reading and playing the guitar. These self-care practices helped him manage his anxiety and improve his overall well-being.

❸ IMPLEMENT EFFECTIVE TIME MANAGEMENT

Effective time management can help us balance work and personal life more efficiently. This involves setting priorities, delegating tasks, and using tools such as calendars and to-do lists to stay organized.

EXAMPLE: Lisa, the project manager, implemented effective time management strategies to balance her work and personal life. She prioritized tasks based on urgency and importance, delegated responsibilities to her team, and used a planner to organize her schedule. Lisa also allocated specific times for family activities, ensuring she spent quality time with her loved ones. These strategies helped Lisa achieve a healthier work–life balance.

❹ SEEK SUPPORT

Seeking support from colleagues, supervisors, and loved ones can help us manage work-related stress. This can involve discussing workload issues with supervisors, seeking mentorship, and leaning on friends and family for emotional support.

EXAMPLE: Mark, the financial analyst, decided to seek support to manage his work-related stress. He discussed his workload with his supervisor, who agreed to redistribute some tasks. Mark also sought mentorship from a senior colleague who provided valuable advice and guidance. Additionally, he leaned on his friends and family for emotional support. This support network helped Mark manage his stress and improve his work–life balance.

❺ CONSIDER FLEXIBLE WORK ARRANGEMENTS

Flexible work arrangements, such as remote work or flexible hours, can help achieve a better work–life balance. These arrangements provide the flexibility to manage work and personal responsibilities more effectively.

EXAMPLE: Sarah, the marketing executive, negotiated a flexible work schedule with her employer. She arranged to work from home two days a week and adjusted her hours to accommodate personal commitments. This flexibility allowed Sarah to manage her workload more efficiently and spend more time with her family. The flexible work arrangement significantly improved Sarah's work–life balance.

❻ PRACTICE MINDFULNESS

Practicing mindfulness can help manage stress and improve focus. Mindfulness involves being present in the moment and can be practiced through meditation, deep-breathing exercises, and mindful activities.

EXAMPLE: Emma, the graphic designer, incorporated mindfulness into her daily routine. She started her day with a short meditation session, practiced deep-breathing exercises during breaks, and engaged in mindful activities such as gardening and painting. These practices helped Emma stay grounded, manage stress, and maintain a healthy work–life balance.

7 DISCONNECT FROM WORK

Regularly disconnecting from work is crucial for mental and emotional well-being. This means taking breaks throughout the day, avoiding work-related activities during personal time, and taking regular vacations.

EXAMPLE: Tom, the software developer, implemented a digital detox strategy to disconnect from work. He set aside specific times during the day to take breaks, avoided checking emails after work hours, and planned regular vacations to unwind. This digital detox helped Tom recharge and maintain a healthier relationship with work.

Maintaining a healthy relationship with work is essential for our mental, emotional, and physical well-being. A balanced work life allows us to perform effectively, nurture personal relationships, and achieve personal and professional growth. Conversely, an unhealthy relationship with work can lead to chronic stress, mental health issues, strained personal relationships, and decreased productivity. By setting boundaries, prioritizing self-care, implementing effective time management, seeking support, considering flexible work arrangements, practicing mindfulness, and regularly disconnecting from work, we can achieve a healthy work–life balance. These strategies ensure that our passion for work remains a source of fulfillment rather than turning into a source of pain.

Ultimately, investing in a healthy relationship with work not only enhances our well-being but also leads to greater job satisfaction and success. By prioritizing balance, we can create a work life that is both rewarding and sustainable, allowing us to thrive both personally and professionally.

CHAPTER 7

NEW YORK: MY BELOVED WHORE

New York is a city that commands attention and adoration in equal measure. To many, it is a glittering metropolis of opportunity and excitement. To me, it is both muse and mistress, a beloved whore that captivates and exploits, seduces and drains. As I walk through its bustling streets, I am reminded of the ways this city can be both lover and leech, offering the world in one hand, and with the other, taking everything.

THE FASHION CAPITAL

New York's fashion scene is a tapestry woven from dreams and desires. The glamour of Fifth Avenue, the bohemian allure of SoHo, and the captivating designs showcased at Fashion Week all paint a picture of a city that is always on the cutting edge of style.

My friend Nikita arrived in New York with stars in her eyes and dreams of becoming the next big name in fashion. Her portfolio was full of sketches that she believed could redefine the industry. The first time she walked into a fashion house on Madison Avenue, she felt like she had stepped into a world where creativity knew no bounds. The air was thick with ambition and the scent of expensive perfume. Models flitted about like gorgeous apparitions, their beauty almost otherworldly. But the reality of the fashion industry in New York soon set in. The competition was fierce, and the demands were relentless. Her designs were scrutinized, her ideas often dismissed. Nikita worked long hours for little pay, desperately trying to prove herself.

The city that had promised so much was now revealing its true nature. It was a demanding lover, insatiable and never fully satisfied. Yet there were moments of sheer ecstasy: the thrill of seeing her designs on the runway, the intoxicating applause, and the fleeting praise from industry giants. These moments were like the tender kisses of a beloved whore, sweet and fleeting, leaving Nikita longing for more. They kept her tied to New York, unable to break free from its seductive hold.

THE MARKETING CAPITAL

In addition to its fashion prowess, New York is the epicenter of marketing and advertising. Madison Avenue is synonymous with the industry, a place where brands are born and dreams are sold. The city's ability to craft narratives and sell them to the world is unparalleled.

My neighbor Courtney's foray into the world of marketing began with an internship at one of the top agencies in the city. The office was a sleek, modern space with floor-to-ceiling windows offering breathtaking views of the skyline. It was a place where ideas flowed as freely as the coffee, and every day felt like a new adventure. But behind the polished facade, there was a brutal reality. The pressure to deliver was immense, the deadlines unforgiving. Creativity was often sacrificed at the altar of profit, and the quest for the next big idea became an endless chase.

Courtney found herself working late into the night, her personal life a distant memory. Despite the hardships, there were moments of triumph: seeing a campaign she had worked on go viral, watching sales soar, and receiving accolades from clients. These were the highs that made the lows bearable. New York, my beloved whore, would give her just enough to keep her hooked, to keep Courtney coming back for more. It was a city that knew how to play the game, offering tantalizing glimpses of success while keeping true fulfillment just out of reach.

THE FINANCE AND INVESTMENT CAPITAL

And then there is the financial heart of New York: Wall Street. The city is a global hub of finance and investment, a place where fortunes are made and lost in the blink of an eye. The energy of Wall Street is electric—a constant buzz of activity and ambition.

My school friend, Tanya, found herself drawn to the world of finance, intrigued by the power and prestige it promised. She landed a job at a major investment firm, working her way up from the bottom. The pace was frenetic, the stakes high. Every decision carried weight; every trade had the potential to change lives. But the demands of the job were all-consuming. The hours were long, the stress unrelenting. Tanya watched her colleagues burn out, their dreams crushed under the weight of expectation. The city that had seemed so full of promise was now a harsh taskmaster, extracting a heavy toll for every success. Yet there were moments of sheer exhilaration: the thrill of closing a big deal, the satisfaction of seeing an investment pay off. These were the moments that made it all worthwhile.

THE INTERSECTION OF FASHION, MARKETING, AND FINANCE

New York's three major industries—fashion, marketing, and finance—are deeply intertwined, each feeding off the other. The fashion industry relies on marketing to promote its brands and reach consumers. Marketing, in turn, depends on finance to fund its campaigns and drive growth. And finance looks to fashion and marketing to create value and generate returns. As I navigated my way through these industries by listening to my friends' stories, I realized that they all shared a common thread: the relentless pursuit of success.

New York, my beloved whore, was a city that demanded everything and gave back just enough to keep you coming back for more. It was a place where dreams were both made and shattered, where the highs were euphoric and the lows devastating. Despite the scary stories, I found myself unable to leave. The city had a hold on me, its seductive allure impossible to resist. The moments of triumph, the fleeting glimpses of success, kept me tied to New York, always striving for more.

But the pursuit of success in New York came at a personal cost. I worked at a startup, and my biggest client was a Fortune 100 pharma company. The long hours, the constant pressure, and the relentless pace all took a toll on my mental and physical health. I found myself becoming more isolated, my relationships suffering. The city that had once felt like a lover now felt like a demanding, unyielding mistress. I began to question whether the pursuit of success was worth the personal sacrifices. Was the fleeting pleasure of professional triumph worth the pain of personal loss? Was the beloved whore that was New York worth the cost?

In time, I realized that the key to surviving and thriving in

New York was finding balance. It was about knowing when to push and when to pull back, when to chase success, and when to prioritize personal well-being. It was about understanding that true fulfillment came not from the external validation of professional achievements but from the internal satisfaction of living a balanced, meaningful life. I began to set boundaries, carving out time for self-care, for relationships, and for the things that brought me joy outside of work. I learned to say no to opportunities that would stretch me too thin to prioritize quality over quantity. I found that by taking care of myself, I was better able to handle the demands of the city, to enjoy the highs and weather the lows.

THE DUALITY OF NEW YORK: A TALE OF GRIT AND GLAMOUR

New York City is a place of stark contrasts, where the grime and grandeur coexist in an intricate dance. It is a city that simultaneously captivates and repels, offering moments of unparalleled beauty alongside scenes of stark reality. This duality is nowhere more evident than in the juxtaposition of its dirty, unsafe corners with its glitzy, glamorous districts.

The Dark Side: Subway Grit and Nighttime Perils

The New York City subway system is both a marvel of engineering and a testament to the city's grittier side. As the lifeline of the city, it transports millions of people daily, yet its conditions can be less than welcoming. Graffiti-covered walls, litter-strewn platforms, and the persistent smell of neglect greet commuters as they navigate the labyrinthine network. For many, the subway's dirt and decay are a daily reminder of the city's darker underbelly.

The stations, often dimly lit and poorly maintained, evoke

a sense of unease. Rats scurry along the tracks, and the noise of trains echoes through the tunnels, creating an atmosphere that can feel more like a scene from a dystopian film than a vital public transportation system. This sense of discomfort is compounded by the knowledge that, particularly late at night, the subway can become a perilous place.

New York's reputation for being unsafe at night, especially for women, adds another layer of darkness to the city's story. Walking alone through certain neighborhoods after sundown can be an anxiety-inducing experience. The threat of crime—muggings, assaults, and harassment—lurks in the shadows. Women often find themselves clutching their bags a little tighter, avoiding deserted streets, and staying hyperaware of their surroundings. This pervasive sense of vulnerability underscores the harsher realities of city life. One can't help but notice the disparity between the city's public spaces and the lives of its inhabitants. The city's frenetic pace and constant noise can feel overwhelming, fostering a sense of isolation even among the throngs of people. This loneliness is a silent companion to many New Yorkers, a stark contrast to the city's outward vibrancy.

The Bright Side: Glamour and Grandeur

Amid the grit, New York's other face shines brightly. The city is home to some of the most iconic and sophisticated cultural landmarks in the world. Take, for example, the splendor of Brooklyn. Known for its picturesque brownstones and vibrant cultural scene, Brooklyn offers a respite from the chaos. Brooklyn Bridge Park provides stunning views of the Manhattan skyline, while the neighborhoods of Williamsburg and Dumbo are havens for artists and young professionals.

Then there are the illustrious events and institutions that

highlight New York's cultural elite. The Met Gala, held at the Metropolitan Museum of Art, is a dazzling annual event that attracts celebrities, fashion icons, and the world's most influential figures. The MoMA (Museum of Modern Art) offers a sanctuary of creativity and innovation, showcasing masterpieces that span the globe and the ages. Tribeca, another gem in New York's crown, is synonymous with luxury and prestige. Home to the Tribeca Film Festival, this neighborhood attracts filmmakers, actors, and cinephiles from around the world. Strolling through its cobblestone streets, one might encounter film stars and directors, lending the area an air of exclusivity and charm.

The West Village, known for its quaint streets and exceptional dining, represents another facet of New York's high life. Renowned restaurants and chic cafés line the streets, offering culinary delights that draw food enthusiasts from far and wide. The area's historic buildings and tree-lined avenues create an enchanting atmosphere, a stark contrast to the city's rougher edges.

Times Square, with its neon lights and bustling energy, epitomizes the city's vibrancy. It is a place where dreams are made, where Broadway shows captivate audiences, and the excitement never dims. The bright lights and constant activity stand in sharp contrast to the dim, deserted subway stations and the shadows of the night.

The Juxtaposition: Beauty and Loneliness

This stark contrast between the city's gritty underbelly and its glamorous facade is what makes New York uniquely captivating. The same city that can feel unsafe and isolating at night transforms into a beacon of culture and sophistication by day. The dirt and decay of the subway give way to the elegance of Tribeca, the artistic haven of MoMA, and the culinary delights of the West

Village. However, even amid the glamour, the underlying zest and loneliness persist. The city's frenzied pace and relentless pursuit of success can create an environment where personal connections are fleeting, and the sense of isolation can be profound. In the midst of a bustling crowd, one can still feel profoundly alone.

New York's duality is a constant reminder of the complexities of urban life. It is a city that demands resilience and adaptability, a place where beauty and the grime coexist in a delicate balance. For every moment of fear and unease, there is a corresponding moment of awe and wonder. The city's ability to inspire and intimidate, to enchant and exhaust, is what makes it truly unique. New York is a city of contrasts. Its dirty train stations and unsafe nighttime streets reflect the harsh realities of urban life, while its cultural landmarks and glamorous neighborhoods showcase its undeniable allure. This juxtaposition is what defines the city's character, making it a place of both profound challenges and extraordinary opportunities. It is a city that tests and rewards, a beloved and demanding muse that continues to captivate those who call it home.

CHAPTER 8

THE DOPAMINE DELULU: UNMASKING THE DELUSION OF INSTANT GRATIFICATION

Dopamine, often referred to as the "feel-good" hormone, plays a critical role in the brain's reward system. It is released during pleasurable activities, reinforcing behaviors and motivating us to repeat them. While dopamine is essential for survival and well-being, our pursuit of the dopamine "hit" can lead to unhealthy behaviors and a cycle of instant gratification. This chapter delves into the phenomenon of "dopamine delulu"—the delusion created by our relentless quest for dopamine—and explores healthier ways to achieve lasting happiness and fulfillment.

UNDERSTANDING DOPAMINE: THE NEUROCHEMICAL BASIS OF PLEASURE

Dopamine is a neurotransmitter that plays several important roles in the brain and body. It is involved in reward, motivation, memory, attention, and even regulating body movements. When we experience something pleasurable, our brain releases dopamine, creating a sensation of happiness and satisfaction. This reward system is crucial for encouraging behaviors that promote survival, such as eating and reproducing. However, dopamine can also reinforce less-healthy behaviors, leading to habits that may have negative long-term consequences. Our modern world is filled with opportunities for quick dopamine hits, from social media and pornography to drugs and unhealthy food. Understanding how dopamine works can help us make more informed choices and avoid the traps of instant gratification.

PORNOGRAPHY AND THE DOPAMINE HIT

One of the most potent sources of dopamine is sexual arousal, and pornography provides a readily accessible way to achieve this. The internet has made pornography more available than ever before, leading to a significant increase in consumption. Each time a person views pornography, their brain releases a surge of dopamine, reinforcing the behavior and creating a cycle of addiction. Over time, the brain becomes desensitized to the dopamine hit from pornography, requiring more extreme content to achieve the same level of satisfaction. This can lead to negative consequences such as decreased interest in real-life sexual relationships, increased risk of erectile dysfunction, and mental health issues like anxiety and depression.

The Ultimate Dopamine Machine

Social media platforms like Facebook, Instagram, and Twitter are designed to maximize user engagement by exploiting our brain's dopamine system. Every like, comment, or share triggers a small release of dopamine, encouraging us to keep scrolling and interacting with content. This design creates a feedback loop that can be difficult to break. The constant quest for social validation through likes and comments can lead to addiction and negatively impact mental health. Studies have shown that excessive social media use is linked to increased feelings of loneliness, anxiety, and depression. The superficial connections and fleeting dopamine hits from social media cannot replace the deeper, more meaningful relationships and experiences that contribute to lasting happiness.

Artificial Dopamine Boosters

Drugs like cocaine, methamphetamine, and marijuana, as well as alcohol, can cause massive releases of dopamine, creating intense feelings of pleasure. However, these substances can also hijack the brain's reward system, leading to addiction. The brain becomes reliant on the artificial dopamine boosts, and natural sources of pleasure—such as social interactions and hobbies—become less satisfying. Addiction to drugs and alcohol can have devastating effects on physical and mental health, relationships, and overall quality of life. The pursuit of the next dopamine hit can over-shadow responsibilities and goals, leading to a downward spiral that is difficult to escape.

The Fast Food of Pleasure

Our society is increasingly geared toward instant gratification, with everything from fast food to online shopping providing quick and easy rewards. These behaviors trigger dopamine release, reinforcing the desire for immediate pleasure. However, the satisfaction from instant gratification is often short-lived, and the long-term consequences can be detrimental. For example, regularly indulging in unhealthy food can lead to weight gain, health problems, and decreased self-esteem. Similarly, impulsive shopping can result in financial stress and clutter.

The cycle of seeking instant gratification can prevent us from achieving long-term goals and finding true fulfillment.

The Facade of Dopamine Delusion

The pursuit of dopamine hits can create a facade of happiness and satisfaction, masking underlying issues and preventing us from addressing the root causes of our behaviors. The temporary pleasure from dopamine hits can distract us from the deeper, more meaningful aspects of life. This delusion can lead to a perpetual state of dissatisfaction, as we constantly chase the next high without ever feeling truly content.

BREAKING FREE FROM THE DOPAMINE DELULU

To break free from the dopamine delusion, we need to adopt healthier ways to achieve lasting happiness and fulfillment. By focusing on activities that provide sustainable sources of pleasure, we can retrain our brains to find joy in more meaningful experiences.

Working Out: Exercise is one of the most effective ways to boost dopamine levels naturally. Physical activity releases endorphins, which interact with dopamine to create a "natural high." Regular exercise can improve mood, reduce stress, and increase overall well-being. Whether it's running, yoga, or lifting weights, finding a form of exercise you enjoy can help you break free from unhealthy habits and achieve lasting happiness.

Practicing Mindfulness: Mindfulness practices such as meditation and deep breathing can help regulate dopamine levels and promote a sense of calm and contentment. By focusing on the present moment and cultivating awareness, you can reduce stress and anxiety, improve concentration, and enhance overall mental health. Regular mindfulness practice can help you develop a healthier relationship with pleasure and avoid the pitfalls of instant gratification.

Traveling: Traveling can provide a wealth of new experiences and opportunities for dopamine release. Exploring new places, meeting new people, and trying new activities can create lasting memories and a sense of fulfillment. Traveling can also help you break out of your routine and develop a broader perspective on life, enhancing your overall well-being.

Writing: Expressing creativity through writing—whether it's journaling, storytelling, or poetry—can be a powerful way to channel emotions and release dopamine. The creative process can provide a sense of accomplishment and satisfaction, helping you develop a deeper connection with yourself and the world around you. Writing can also be a therapeutic tool, allowing you to process and understand your thoughts and feelings.

Playing with Your Pet: Spending time with pets can boost dopamine levels and provide a sense of unconditional love and joy. The bond between humans and animals is a powerful source of comfort and happiness. Playing with your pet, taking them for walks, or simply cuddling can improve your mood and reduce stress.

Engaging in Healthier Habits: Developing healthier habits—such as eating nutritious food, getting enough sleep, and fostering meaningful relationships—can create a strong foundation for lasting happiness. By prioritizing activities that promote overall well-being, you can build a more fulfilling and balanced life.

The dopamine delusion or "dopamine delulu" is a trap that many of us fall into in our quest for instant gratification. While dopamine is a vital part of our brain's reward system, relying on quick dopamine hits from unhealthy behaviors can lead to a cycle of addiction and dissatisfaction. By understanding the nature of dopamine and adopting healthier ways to achieve pleasure, we can break free from this delusion and find true, lasting happiness.

Working out, practicing mindfulness, traveling, writing, playing with pets, and engaging in healthier habits are all ways to supercharge our dopamine levels naturally. These activities provide sustainable sources of pleasure and contribute to overall well-being. By focusing on meaningful experiences and developing a healthier relationship with pleasure, we can create a more fulfilling and balanced life. In the end, the key to breaking free from the dopamine delusion is to prioritize activities that promote long-term happiness and well-being. By making conscious choices and embracing healthier habits, we can achieve a deeper sense of fulfillment and avoid the traps of instant gratification. The journey from pain to pleasure is one that requires mindfulness, patience, and a commitment to living a balanced and meaningful life.

CHAPTER 9

SCORING GREEN: A THRILLING TALE OF MARIJUANA, CULTURE, AND CONTROVERSY

Jenna Lee sat in her small, dimly lit apartment in a state of agitation. The once-thriving entrepreneur, who had built her tech startup from the ground up, now found herself engulfed in a whirlwind of stress and anxiety. Her company was on the brink of collapse, and the relentless pressure had taken a toll on her mental health. Desperation led her to seek solace in an unconventional remedy: marijuana. Living in a state where marijuana was not easily accessible, Jenna faced a significant challenge. Despite its proven benefits for managing stress and anxiety, obtaining marijuana legally was not an option. Determined to find relief, Jenna embarked on a daring journey to score some weed, knowing the risks but convinced of its necessity.

THE QUEST BEGINS

Jenna's first step was to reach out to an old friend, Marcus, who had connections in the underground marijuana market. Marcus, a musician with a laid-back demeanor, had always been a staunch advocate for the legalization of marijuana. He understood Jenna's plight and agreed to help her out. They arranged to meet at a secluded coffee shop downtown.

The place was a front for various illicit activities, hidden in plain sight. Jenna felt a mix of excitement and apprehension as she walked in, scanning the room for Marcus. He waved her over to a corner booth, his expression serious. "Are you sure you want to do this?" Marcus asked, his voice low and cautious.

"I have no choice," Jenna replied, her resolve unwavering. "I need something to help me cope."

Marcus nodded and handed her a slip of paper with an address scribbled on it. "Go to this location tonight. Ask for Greenman. He'll know what you need."

INTO THE UNDERWORLD

That evening, Jenna found herself in a rundown part of town, standing in front of a nondescript building. Her heart raced as she knocked on the door, which creaked open to reveal a burly man with a suspicious glare. "I'm here to see Greenman," she said, trying to keep her voice steady. The man scrutinized her for a moment before stepping aside, allowing her to enter. Jenna was led through a maze of dimly lit corridors, the air thick with the smell of marijuana. Finally, she was ushered into a small room where a tall, wiry man sat behind a desk, surrounded by potted cannabis plants. "Greenman, I presume?" Jenna ventured.

The man chuckled, his eyes twinkling. "That's me. And you must be Jenna. Marcus said you were in need." Jenna explained her situation, her words tumbling out in a rush. Greenman listened patiently, nodding in understanding. "You're not alone, Jenna. Many people turn to marijuana for relief. But remember, it comes with risks," he warned. "The law is not on our side."

"I understand," Jenna replied. "I just need something to help me get through this rough patch."

Greenman handed her a small, discreet package. "This should do the trick. Use it wisely."

THE BENEFITS OF MARIJUANA

As Jenna left the building, she couldn't help but reflect on the potential benefits of the plant she now held in her hands. Marijuana, known scientifically as cannabis, has been used for centuries for its medicinal properties. It has been shown to alleviate symptoms of anxiety, depression, chronic pain, and various other ailments. For individuals with severe illnesses such as cancer, multiple sclerosis, and epilepsy, marijuana can offer significant relief. Its active compounds, THC and CBD, interact with the body's endocannabinoids system, helping to reduce pain, inflammation, and nausea. Many patients have reported improved quality of life and better management of their symptoms with the use of medical marijuana.

A CULTURAL HISTORY

Marijuana's significance extends beyond its medicinal benefits. It has played a vital role in various cultures throughout history. In Hinduism, the god Shiva is often depicted smoking marijuana, which is believed to help him meditate and connect with the divine. The plant is used in religious ceremonies and traditional medicine, symbolizing both spirituality and healing. In ancient China, cannabis was used for its fiber to make textiles and as a medicine to treat various ailments. Similarly, in ancient Egypt, marijuana was used for medicinal purposes, including pain relief and anti-inflammatory treatments. Indigenous cultures in the Americas have also utilized marijuana for its therapeutic properties and as a part of their spiritual practices.

THE PUSH FOR LEGALIZATION

Despite its historical and medicinal significance, marijuana remains illegal in many parts of the world. The push for legalization is gaining momentum, driven by growing evidence of its benefits and changing public perceptions. Advocates argue that legalizing marijuana would allow for better regulation, ensuring product safety and quality while reducing the black market and related criminal activities. Legalization could also provide economic benefits, including job creation and tax revenue. States that have legalized marijuana, such as New York, Colorado, and California, have seen significant economic growth and increased funding for public services through marijuana taxes.

THE OPPOSITION

The path to legalization is fraught with obstacles. One of the primary reasons marijuana remains illegal is the influence of the pharmaceutical industry. Big Pharma has a vested interest in keeping marijuana illegal, as it poses a threat to their profits. Marijuana offers a natural alternative to many prescription medications, potentially reducing the demand for costly pharmaceuticals. The pharmaceutical industry's lobbying efforts have played a significant role in shaping drug policies, creating barriers to marijuana legalization. They argue that marijuana lacks the rigorous testing and standardization required for medical use, despite growing evidence of its efficacy.

JENNA'S REVELATION

Back in her apartment, Jenna carefully unpacked the marijuana Greenman had given her. She knew that using it carried risks, but she also believed in its potential to help her through her current crisis. As she took her first puff, she felt a wave of relaxation wash over her, the tension in her body easing. Over the next few days, Jenna found herself able to focus more clearly on her work. The marijuana helped her manage her anxiety, allowing her to approach her problems with a calmer mindset. She began to see a path forward for her struggling startup, making strategic decisions that had previously seemed overwhelming.

A NEW PERSPECTIVE

Jenna's experience with marijuana opened her eyes to its potential benefits and the broader issues surrounding its legality. She became an advocate for legalization, speaking out about her own journey and the need for more compassionate drug policies. She connected with other entrepreneurs and professionals who had also turned to marijuana for relief, forming a support network that advocated for change. She learned about the benefits of marijuana beyond her own experience, such as its potential to help people with severe illnesses. For cancer patients undergoing chemotherapy, marijuana can reduce nausea and stimulate appetite, improving their overall quality of life. People with chronic pain conditions such as fibromyalgia and arthritis have found relief through medical marijuana, allowing them to reduce or eliminate their reliance on opioid painkillers.

The Case for Legalization

Jenna's newfound passion for marijuana advocacy led her to

delve deeper into the arguments for legalization. She discovered that legalizing marijuana could have numerous societal benefits, including reducing the burden on the criminal justice system. Currently, a significant number of arrests and incarcerations are related to marijuana possession and use, disproportionately affecting minority communities. Legalization would also allow for better regulation and quality control, ensuring that consumers have access to safe and standardized products. It would reduce the influence of the black market, cutting off a major source of revenue for criminal organizations. Furthermore, the tax revenue generated from legal marijuana sales could be used to fund public services, such as education and healthcare.

The Path Forward

Despite the many compelling arguments for legalization, Jenna understood that change would not come easily. It would require a concerted effort from advocates, policymakers, and the public to overcome the entrenched interests of the pharmaceutical industry and other opponents. She became involved in grassroots organizations that were working to change marijuana laws, attending rallies, and lobbying lawmakers. She shared her story with the media, hoping to shift public perception and build support for legalization. Jenna's journey was not just about scoring weed; it was about fighting for a future where people could access the medicine they needed without fear of legal repercussions.

The Power of Advocacy

Jenna's experience with marijuana highlighted the complex and often controversial nature of the plant. Her journey from a distressed entrepreneur seeking relief to a passionate advocate for legalization underscored the transformative potential of marijuana. While the path to legalization is fraught with challenges, the growing body of evidence supporting its benefits and the changing public attitudes offer hope for a future where marijuana is recognized for its medicinal and cultural significance.

In the end, Jenna's story is a testament to the power of personal experience and advocacy. By speaking out and sharing her journey, she contributed to the broader movement for marijuana legalization, helping to pave the way for a more compassionate and informed approach to drug policy. As society continues to evolve, the hope is that marijuana will be fully recognized for its potential to heal and improve lives, breaking free from the stigma and legal constraints that have long surrounded it.

CHAPTER 10

THE UNDERRATED ADDICTION: HOW WORKING OUT CAN BE THE BEST DRUG FOR ENTREPRENEURS

In today's fast-paced world, where stress and mental health challenges are becoming increasingly prevalent, entrepreneurs face unique pressures. Building and running a business demands resilience, creativity, and the ability to handle immense stress. While some turn to unhealthy habits like excessive caffeine, alcohol, or more dangerous substances to cope, there is a healthier, more beneficial addiction that often goes overlooked: working out.

THE SCIENCE OF EXERCISE AND MENTAL HEALTH

Before diving into the benefits of working out, it's essential to understand the science behind how exercise affects our mental health. Physical activity triggers the release of various neurotransmitters and hormones that play a crucial role in mood regulation and stress relief.

🏵 ENDORPHINS

Often referred to as "feel-good" hormones, endorphins are released during physical activity, leading to a state of euphoria commonly known as the "runner's high." This natural high can significantly improve mood and reduce feelings of pain and discomfort.

🏵 SEROTONIN

Regular exercise boosts serotonin levels. Serotonin helps regulate mood, sleep, and appetite, and higher levels of serotonin are associated with lower levels of depression and anxiety.

🏵 DOPAMINE

Exercise increases dopamine production, a neurotransmitter linked to pleasure, motivation, and reward. Enhanced dopamine levels can lead to improved focus and a sense of accomplishment.

🏵 NOREPINEPHRINE

Norepinephrine, a hormone released during exercise, enhances alertness, attention, and energy levels. It helps the brain respond better to stress, improving an individual's ability to handle pressure and anxiety.

🏵 BDNF (BRAIN-DERIVED NEUROTROPHIC FACTOR)

Exercise stimulates the production of BDNF, which supports brain health by promoting the growth and maintenance of neurons. Higher BDNF levels are associated with improved cognitive function and reduced risk of neurodegenerative diseases.

THE BENEFITS OF WORKING OUT FOR ENTREPRENEURS

1 STRESS REDUCTION

Entrepreneurs often deal with high levels of stress due to the demands of their roles. Exercise is one of the most effective ways to combat stress. The physical exertion helps to reduce cortisol levels (the primary stress hormone) in the body, providing a natural way to alleviate tension and anxiety.

EXAMPLE Richard Branson, the founder of Virgin Group, attributes much of his success to his active lifestyle. He frequently engages in physical activities like kitesurfing, swimming, and tennis, which help him manage stress and stay focused on his entrepreneurial endeavors.

2 IMPROVED MENTAL CLARITY AND FOCUS

Exercise enhances cognitive function by increasing blood flow to the brain, promoting neurogenesis (the creation of new brain cells), and improving memory and learning capabilities. For entrepreneurs, this means better decision-making, problem-solving, and creativity.

EXAMPLE Mark Zuckerberg, cofounder and CEO of Meta (formerly Facebook), incorporates regular exercise into his routine, including running and martial arts. He believes that staying physically active helps him maintain mental clarity and make better decisions.

3 ENHANCED MOOD AND EMOTIONAL RESILIENCE

The release of endorphins and serotonin during exercise can significantly boost mood and emotional resilience. Entrepreneurs often face setbacks and failures, and maintaining a positive outlook is crucial for long-term success. Regular physical activity can help entrepreneurs stay motivated and resilient in the face of challenges.

EXAMPLE Arianna Huffington, founder of *HuffPost* (formerly *The Huffington Post*), practices yoga and meditation to maintain her mental well-being. These practices help her stay emotionally resilient and focused on her goals.

❹ BETTER SLEEP QUALITY

Quality sleep is essential for cognitive function, emotional regulation, and overall health. Exercise has been shown to improve sleep quality by regulating sleep patterns and reducing symptoms of insomnia. Entrepreneurs who prioritize physical activity are more likely to enjoy restful sleep, leading to increased productivity and better mental health.

EXAMPLE Jeff Bezos, founder and former president and CEO of Amazon, emphasizes the importance of sleep and includes regular exercise in his routine. He believes that good sleep and physical activity contribute to his effectiveness as a leader.

❺ INCREASED ENERGY LEVELS

While it may seem counterintuitive, expending energy through exercise actually increases overall energy levels. Regular physical activity boosts stamina and reduces feelings of fatigue, enabling entrepreneurs to sustain their productivity throughout the day.

EXAMPLE Oprah Winfrey incorporates regular exercise into her daily routine, including activities like hiking, strength training, and running. She credits her high energy levels and sustained productivity to her commitment to physical fitness.

🌼 IMPROVED SELF-DISCIPLINE AND TIME MANAGEMENT

Consistent exercise requires self-discipline and effective time management, skills that are directly transferable to entrepreneurship. Establishing a regular workout routine can help entrepreneurs develop these qualities, leading to better organization and productivity in their business endeavors.

EXAMPLE Tim Ferriss, author of *The 4-Hour Workweek*, is known for his disciplined approach to fitness. He believes that the self-discipline gained from regular exercise translates into increased productivity and efficiency in his professional life.

🌼 NETWORKING AND RELATIONSHIP BUILDING

Engaging in physical activities can also provide opportunities for networking and relationship building. Entrepreneurs can connect with like-minded individuals through fitness classes, sports clubs, and other exercise-related events, expanding their professional network and creating valuable business connections.

EXAMPLE Many business leaders participate in golf, tennis, or running clubs, where they can network and build relationships with potential clients, partners, and investors.

WHY EXERCISE IS THE BEST ADDICTION

🌼 NATURAL AND SUSTAINABLE

Unlike drugs or other unhealthy coping mechanisms, exercise is a natural and sustainable way to enhance mental and physical health. It doesn't carry the risk of addiction, dependency, or negative side effects associated with substances like alcohol or drugs.

EXAMPLE While some entrepreneurs might turn to stimulants like caffeine or even prescription medications to boost productivity, these can lead to dependency and negative health consequences. In contrast, exercise provides a healthy, sustainable way to maintain high energy levels and mental clarity.

❷ HOLISTIC BENEFITS

Exercise offers a wide range of holistic benefits, addressing not just mental health but also physical well-being. Regular physical activity can reduce the risk of chronic diseases, improve cardiovascular health, enhance immune function, and promote a healthy weight.

EXAMPLE Entrepreneurs who prioritize exercise are more likely to experience overall health improvements, reducing the likelihood of health-related disruptions to their business activities.

❸ POSITIVE IMPACT ON SELF-ESTEEM

Regular exercise can significantly improve self-esteem and body image. Achieving fitness goals and seeing physical progress can boost confidence and self-worth, which can be particularly beneficial for entrepreneurs facing constant scrutiny and pressure.

EXAMPLE Dwayne "The Rock" Johnson, who maintains a rigorous workout routine, often speaks about the confidence and self-esteem gained from regular exercise.

❹ HEALTHY COPING MECHANISM

Exercise serves as a healthy coping mechanism for managing stress, anxiety, and other mental health challenges. Instead of turning to unhealthy habits, entrepreneurs can use physical activity to channel their energy and emotions in a productive way.

EXAMPLE: Anna Wintour, editor-in-chief of Vogue, starts her day with a game of tennis. This routine helps her manage the stress and demands of her high-pressure job.

❺ POSITIVE ROLE MODELING

Entrepreneurs who prioritize fitness and well-being can serve as positive role models for their employees, clients, and the broader community. Demonstrating a commitment to health and wellness can inspire others to adopt similar habits, creating a positive ripple effect.

EXAMPLE: Michelle Obama, through her Let's Move! campaign, encouraged people across the United States to prioritize physical activity and healthy eating, serving as a role model for millions.

TYPES OF EXERCISE FOR ENTREPRENEURS

There are various types of exercise that entrepreneurs can incorporate into their routines, each offering unique benefits. Here are a few options:

❶ CARDIOVASCULAR EXERCISE

Cardiovascular exercise such as running, cycling, or swimming is excellent for improving heart health, increasing stamina, and boosting mood. It can be easily integrated into a busy schedule with activities like morning runs or lunchtime bike rides.

Jack Dorsey, cofounder and former CEO of Twitter, is known for his commitment to running. He often takes morning jogs, which help him clear his mind and prepare for the day ahead.

❷ STRENGTH TRAINING

Strength training, including weight lifting and bodyweight exercises, is crucial for building muscle, improving bone density, and enhancing overall strength. It can also boost metabolism and help maintain a healthy weight.

Jessica Alba, actress and founder of The Honest Company, incorporates strength training into her fitness routine to maintain her health and energy levels.

❸ YOGA AND PILATES

Yoga and Pilates focus on flexibility, balance, and core strength. These practices also incorporate mindfulness and breathing techniques, making them excellent for reducing stress and improving mental clarity.

Russell Simmons, cofounder of Def Jam Recordings, practices yoga and meditation regularly, which he credits for helping him maintain balance and focus in his entrepreneurial endeavors.

❹ HIGH-INTENSITY INTERVAL TRAINING (HIIT)

HIIT workouts involve short bursts of intense exercise followed by periods of rest or low-intensity exercise. These workouts are time-efficient and effective for improving cardiovascular fitness, burning calories, and building strength.

EXAMPLE Entrepreneur and fitness enthusiast Joe Wicks, also known as The Body Coach, popularized HIIT workouts through his online fitness programs, helping millions achieve their fitness goals.

❀ OUTDOOR ACTIVITIES

Engaging in outdoor activities like hiking, rock climbing, or kayaking can provide a refreshing break from the daily grind while offering the physical and mental benefits of exercise. Being in nature can also enhance mood and reduce stress.

EXAMPLE Blake Mycoskie, founder of TOMS Shoes, enjoys outdoor activities like surfing and hiking, which help him stay grounded and connected to nature.

OVERCOMING BARRIERS TO EXERCISE

Despite the numerous benefits, many entrepreneurs struggle to incorporate regular exercise into their busy schedules. Here are some strategies to overcome common barriers:

❶ TIME MANAGEMENT

One of the most common excuses for not exercising is a lack of time. Entrepreneurs can overcome this barrier by scheduling workouts like any other important meeting or task. Even short fifteen- to thirty-minute sessions can be effective if done consistently.

EXAMPLE Jeff Weiner, former CEO of LinkedIn, schedules time for exercise in his daily calendar to ensure it remains a priority.

❷ FINDING ENJOYABLE ACTIVITIES

Exercise should be enjoyable, not a chore. Finding physical activities that you genuinely enjoy can make it easier to stick with a fitness routine. Experiment with different types of exercise until you find what works best for you.

EXAMPLE: Serena Williams, professional tennis player and entrepreneur, enjoys a variety of physical activities, including dancing and swimming, in addition to her tennis training.

❸ SETTING REALISTIC GOALS

Setting realistic and achievable fitness goals can provide motivation and a sense of accomplishment. Start with small, manageable goals and gradually increase the intensity and duration of your workouts.

EXAMPLE: Richard Branson sets realistic fitness goals, such as participating in a marathon or completing a challenging hike, which keeps him motivated and focused on his physical health.

❹ ACCOUNTABILITY AND SUPPORT

Having a workout partner or joining a fitness group can provide accountability and support. Sharing your fitness journey with others can make it more enjoyable and help you stay committed to your goals.

EXAMPLE: Entrepreneurs like Sheryl Sandberg and Mark Zuckerberg have been known to work out together, providing mutual support and accountability.

Working out is an underrated addiction that offers immense benefits for entrepreneurs. From reducing stress and improving mental clarity to enhancing mood and emotional resilience, exercise can be a powerful tool for managing the unique challenges of entrepreneurship. By prioritizing physical activity, entrepreneurs can boost their overall well-being, enhance their productivity, and inspire others to do the same. Instead of turning to unhealthy coping mechanisms, entrepreneurs should embrace exercise as a natural and sustainable way to improve their mental and physical health. Whether through cardiovascular exercise, strength training, yoga, or outdoor activities, there are countless ways to incorporate fitness into a busy lifestyle. By overcoming common barriers and finding enjoyable activities, entrepreneurs can make exercise a consistent and rewarding part of their daily routine. Ultimately, the benefits of exercise extend far beyond physical health, providing a holistic approach to well-being that can transform both personal and professional lives. So, if you're looking for a healthy addiction that can enhance your entrepreneurial journey, look no further than the power of working out.

PART III
AROUSAL

CHAPTER 11

HOW TO BE A MILLIONAIRE IN TWELVE MONTHS!

Becoming a millionaire in twelve months is an ambitious goal, but with the right strategy, dedication, and mindset, it is achievable. While the path to success can vary greatly depending on the profession and approach, there are several key methods that can pave the way to financial success within a year. Here, we explore various avenues, from traditional businesses to digital entrepreneurship, that can help you achieve this milestone.

ENTREPRENEURSHIP (STARTING A SCALABLE BUSINESS)

Launching a business with high growth potential is one of the most effective ways to amass significant wealth quickly. Focus on industries with rapid growth and scalability, such as technology, e-commerce, and healthcare. A well-crafted business plan, a unique value proposition, and effective marketing can help you capture market share swiftly.

EXAMPLE: Launching a tech startup with a revolutionary app or service that addresses a common problem can attract investors and customers quickly. With the right execution, it's possible to achieve exponential growth and significant revenue within a year.

REAL ESTATE INVESTMENT

Flipping Houses

Buying, renovating, and selling properties at a profit, also known as flipping houses, can yield substantial returns in a short period. Key to success in this area is identifying undervalued properties, managing renovation costs effectively, and selling at a premium.

EXAMPLE Purchasing distressed properties in a high-demand area, renovating them to add value, and selling them at a higher price can generate significant profits. With multiple successful flips, reaching the millionaire mark is feasible.

Real Estate Development

Developing residential or commercial properties can also be a lucrative venture. This requires substantial initial capital and expertise in property development and market trends.

EXAMPLE Investing in the development of a small apartment complex in an emerging neighborhood can lead to substantial returns upon sale or rental of the units.

STOCK MARKET INVESTMENT

Day Trading

Day trading involves buying and selling stocks within the same trading day to capitalize on small price movements. This method requires deep market knowledge, technical analysis skills, and the ability to make quick decisions.

EXAMPLE A disciplined day trader can leverage market volatility to make significant profits. Using sophisticated trading tools and strategies, it's possible to accumulate wealth rapidly.

Investing in High-Growth Stocks

Investing in stocks of companies with high growth potential can also yield substantial returns. This approach requires thorough research and understanding of market trends and company fundamentals.

EXAMPLE: Early investment in tech giants like Nvidia, Amazon, Tesla, or emerging startups with innovative products can result in massive returns as these companies grow.

DIGITAL ENTREPRENEURSHIP

E-Commerce

Starting an online store can be a highly profitable venture. Identifying a niche market, sourcing unique products, and leveraging digital marketing strategies can help you build a successful e-commerce business.

EXAMPLE: Creating a brand around a trending product or a subscription box service can attract a loyal customer base and drive sales rapidly.

Dropshipping

Dropshipping allows you to sell products without holding inventory. Partnering with suppliers who handle inventory and shipping can minimize initial costs and risks.

EXAMPLE: Setting up a dropshipping store on a platform like

Shopify, focusing on high-demand products, and using targeted advertising can generate substantial revenue.

DIGITAL CONTENT CREATION

YouTube and Podcasting

Creating content on platforms like YouTube and podcasting can be a lucrative endeavor. Monetizing through ads, sponsorships, and merchandise sales can lead to significant earnings.

EXAMPLE Building a YouTube channel around a popular niche such as personal finance, travel, or technology and growing a large subscriber base can generate substantial ad revenue and sponsorship deals.

Online Courses and E-books

Creating and selling online courses or e-books on subjects you are knowledgeable about can be a great way to generate passive income.

EXAMPLE Developing a comprehensive online course on a high-demand skill such as coding, digital marketing, or entre-preneurship, and marketing it effectively, can result in sub-stantial sales.

PROFESSIONAL SERVICES

Consulting

Offering consulting services in your area of expertise can be highly profitable. Businesses are often willing to pay a premium for expert advice that can drive growth or solve critical problems.

EXAMPLE: A marketing consultant helping small businesses scale their operations through effective digital marketing strategies can charge high fees for their services.

Freelancing

High-demand skills such as software development, graphic design, and copywriting can be leveraged to earn substantial income through freelancing platforms.

EXAMPLE: A software developer offering specialized services on platforms like Upwork or Fiverr can attract high-paying clients and complete multiple projects within a year to reach their financial goals.

INNOVATIVE TECHNOLOGIES

Cryptocurrency Trading

Cryptocurrency trading can offer significant returns, though it comes with high risk. Understanding market dynamics and employing strategic trading can yield substantial profits.

EXAMPLE: Investing in promising cryptocurrencies during their early stages and taking advantage of market surges can lead to impressive returns.

Developing Blockchain Solutions

Creating blockchain-based applications and solutions for various industries can attract significant investment and generate revenue quickly.

EXAMPLE: Launching a decentralized finance (DeFi) platform that offers unique financial services can attract users and investors, leading to rapid growth.

While becoming a millionaire in twelve months is a challenging goal, it is not impossible with the right approach. Whether you choose to start a scalable business, invest in real estate or the stock market, create digital content, offer professional services, or leverage innovative technologies, success hinges on dedication, strategic planning, and the ability to capitalize on opportunities. Remember, each path requires a unique set of skills and resources, so choose the one that aligns best with your strengths and interests. With persistence and a bit of luck, reaching the millionaire milestone is within your grasp.

CHAPTER 12

SEX

From ancient practices to modern phenomena, sex has always been a fundamental aspect of human life—shaping societies, cultures, and personal relationships throughout history. From ancient practices documented in texts like the *Kama Sutra* to contemporary explorations of sexuality, the ways humans engage in sex have evolved dramatically. Here, we explore the history of sex, the prevalence of sex crimes, the various forms of sexual activities practiced around the world, and the cultural significance of sex. Additionally, we delve into the importance of sexual education, the benefits of a healthy sex life, and the impact of sexual satisfaction on personal and professional relationships.

ANCIENT PRACTICES AND TEXTS

Sexuality in ancient times was often intertwined with religious and cultural practices. Ancient civilizations such as the Greeks, Romans, Egyptians, and Indians had rich sexual traditions that were reflected in their art, literature, and societal norms.

The Kama Sutra

One of the most influential texts on sexuality is the *Kama Sutra*, an ancient Indian treatise written by Vātsyāyana. Composed between 400 BCE and 200 CE, the *Kama Sutra* is more than just a manual for sexual positions; it is a comprehensive guide to living a fulfilling and balanced life. The text covers a wide range of topics, including the nature of love, the duties of a wife and husband, and the appropriate conduct for men and women. However, it is best known for its detailed descriptions of various sexual positions and techniques, emphasizing the importance of mutual pleasure and connection. The *Kama Sutra*'s influence has been profound, shaping sexual practices and attitudes not only in India but around the world. It celebrates sex as an art form and a vital aspect of human experience, encouraging people to explore their desires and enhance their intimate relationships.

Sex in Ancient Greece and Rome

In ancient Greece and Rome, sex was an integral part of daily life and often depicted in their art and mythology. The Greeks in particular had a more fluid understanding of sexuality, and relationships between men and young boys (pederasty) were socially accepted as a form of mentorship and education. Women, on the other hand, were often relegated to the domestic sphere, with their sexual roles confined to marriage and procreation. The Romans adopted many of the Greeks' attitudes toward sex but were also known for their extravagant and often debauched sexual practices. Orgies, a common feature of Roman society, were elaborate gatherings where participants engaged in various sexual activities. These events highlighted the Romans' pursuit of pleasure and their belief in the liberating power of sex.

THE DARK SIDE: SEX CRIMES

Despite the celebration of sex in many cultures, there has always been a darker side to human sexuality—sex crimes. These crimes, which include rape, sexual assault, and exploitation, have devastating effects on victims and are pervasive across all societies.

Historical Context

Sex crimes have a long and troubling history. In ancient times, women were often viewed as property, and their sexual autonomy was severely restricted. Rape was not only a crime against the woman but also a crime against her husband or father, as it was seen as a violation of their property rights. This patriarchal view persisted for centuries, leading to the systemic oppression of women and the normalization of sexual violence.

Modern-Day Challenges

Today, sex crimes remain a significant issue, with many cases going unreported due to stigma, fear, and victim-blaming. The #MeToo movement, which gained global traction in 2017, brought much-needed attention to the prevalence of sexual harassment and assault, encouraging survivors to speak out and seek justice. Despite these advancements, the fight against sex crimes continues, requiring concerted efforts from governments, communities, and individuals to support victims and create safer environments.

THE DIVERSITY OF SEXUAL PRACTICES

Sexual practices vary widely across cultures and individuals, reflecting the diverse ways humans experience and express their sexuality. Here, we explore some common forms of sexual activities and their cultural significance.

Solo Sex

Masturbation, or self-pleasure, is a natural and healthy sexual activity that allows individuals to explore their bodies and understand their sexual preferences. Despite historical taboos and misconceptions, modern science recognizes the benefits of masturbation, including stress relief, improved mood, and enhanced sexual satisfaction.

Twosomes, Threesomes, and Orgies

The most common form of sexual activity is between two partners, often referred to as twosomes. This can involve a wide range of activities, from kissing and touching to intercourse. The key to a satisfying sexual relationship is communication and mutual consent, ensuring both partners feel comfortable and respected.

Threesomes and orgies involve multiple participants and can offer unique and exciting sexual experiences. Threesomes typically involve three people, while orgies include larger groups. These activities require clear communication, consent, and boundaries to ensure a positive experience for everyone involved. While not for everyone, some people find that group sex enhances their sexual pleasure and intimacy with their partners.

Exploring Kinks

BDSM stands for bondage, discipline, dominance and submission, and sadomasochism. This sexual practice involves consensual power dynamics, where one partner takes on a dominant role, and the other assumes a submissive role. BDSM can include activities such as bondage, spanking, role-playing, and sensory deprivation. The key to safe and enjoyable BDSM experiences is trust, communication, and mutual consent.

Wild Forms of Sex

Beyond BDSM, people engage in various wild and unconventional forms of sex. These can include public sex, exhibitionism, voyeurism, and other fetishes. While these activities can add excitement and novelty to one's sex life, it's important to ensure that all parties involved are consenting adults and that the activities do not harm anyone.

THE INFLUENCE OF THE KAMA SUTRA AND INDIAN CULTURE

The *Kama Sutra*'s impact extends far beyond India, influencing sexual practices and attitudes worldwide. Its emphasis on mutual pleasure, respect, and connection resonates with people from diverse backgrounds, encouraging them to explore and celebrate their sexuality.

Indian Culture and Global Phenomenon

Indian culture has a rich history of sexual openness and exploration, as evidenced by ancient texts like the *Kama Sutra* and the erotic sculptures of Khajuraho. These cultural artifacts highlight the importance of sex in Indian society, not just as a means of procreation but as a source of joy and spiritual connection. The global influence of Indian culture is evident in the widespread interest in practices like yoga and meditation, which promote a holistic approach to well-being, including sexual health. By embracing the principles of the *Kama Sutra* and other ancient traditions, people worldwide can learn to appreciate sex as a vital and enriching part of life.

THE IMPORTANCE OF SEXUAL SATISFACTION FOR ENTREPRENEURS

For entrepreneurs, maintaining a healthy and satisfying sex life can be crucial for overall well-being and success. The demands of running a business can lead to high levels of stress and burnout, making it essential to find effective ways to relax and recharge.

Sex as Stress Relief

Sex, including masturbation and intimate activities with a partner, can be a powerful stress reliever. The physical and emotional benefits of sex, such as the release of endorphins and oxytocin, can improve mood, reduce anxiety, and enhance overall mental health. For entrepreneurs, these benefits can translate into increased creativity, productivity, and resilience.

Building Strong Relationships

Having a partner who is good in bed and with whom you share a strong sexual connection can significantly impact the quality of a relationship or marriage. Sexual satisfaction fosters emotional intimacy and trust, creating a solid foundation for a supportive and loving partnership. For entrepreneurs, a stable and fulfilling relationship can provide the emotional support needed to navigate the challenges of their professional lives.

THE IMPORTANCE OF SEX EDUCATION

Comprehensive sex education is essential for promoting healthy sexual development and preventing sex crimes. Educating children and teenagers about sex, consent, and healthy relationships can empower them to make informed choices and respect others' boundaries.

Sex education can reduce the incidence of teenage pregnancies, sexually transmitted infections (STIs), and sexual violence. By providing accurate information and fostering open conversations about sex, we can create a more informed and respectful society.

Challenges and Controversies

Despite the clear benefits, sex education remains a contentious issue in many parts of the world. Cultural and religious beliefs often influence the content and availability of sex education programs, leading to disparities in the quality of education. Advocates must continue to push for comprehensive and inclusive sex education to ensure that all young people have the knowledge and skills they need to navigate their sexual lives safely and responsibly.

THE BENEFITS OF GOOD SEX FOR HUMANITY

A healthy and satisfying sex life can have numerous benefits for individuals and society as a whole. Good sex contributes to physical and mental health, strengthens relationships, and enhances overall quality of life.

Physical Health

Regular sexual activity has been linked to various health benefits, including improved cardiovascular health, a stronger immune system, and better sleep. The physical exertion of sex can also be a form of exercise, helping to maintain a healthy weight and reduce the risk of chronic diseases.

Mental Health

Sexual satisfaction can have a profound impact on mental health. The release of endorphins and oxytocin during sex can improve mood, reduce stress, and alleviate symptoms of anxiety and depression. Additionally, the emotional intimacy and connection that come with a fulfilling sex life can enhance overall well-being and life satisfaction.

Strengthening Relationships

Good sex is a vital component of a healthy relationship. It fosters emotional intimacy, trust, and communication between partners, creating a strong foundation for a lasting and fulfilling partnership. Couples who are sexually satisfied are more likely to have positive interactions, resolve conflicts effectively, and support each other through life's challenges.

THE LEGALIZATION DEBATE

The question of whether to legalize various aspects of sex, such as sex work and certain sexual practices, remains a complex and contentious issue. Proponents argue that legalization could provide better protection and regulation, ensuring the safety and rights of those involved. Opponents, however, often cite moral and ethical concerns.

Advocates argue that legalizing and regulating sex work could reduce the risks associated with the underground market, such as exploitation, violence, and health hazards. Legalization could also provide sex workers with legal protections, access to healthcare, and the ability to work in safer conditions. Opponents, however, argue that legalization may not fully address the underlying issues of exploitation and may perpetuate the objectification of individuals. The debate continues, with some countries and states adopting different approaches to address the complexities of sex work.

EMBRACING SEXUALITY FOR A BETTER FUTURE

Sex is an integral part of human life, shaping our identities, relationships, and societies. From the ancient teachings of the *Kama Sutra* to modern explorations of sexuality, the ways humans engage in sex have evolved, reflecting our diverse experiences and desires. Understanding the history and significance of sex, addressing the dark side of sex crimes, and embracing the diversity of sexual practices can help create a more informed and respectful society.

Comprehensive sex education is essential for empowering young people to make informed choices and fostering healthy relationships. For entrepreneurs and individuals alike, maintaining a healthy and satisfying sex life is crucial for overall well-being and success. Good sex can enhance physical and mental health, strengthen relationships, and contribute to a fulfilling and balanced life. As we continue to explore and celebrate our sexuality, it is important to advocate for policies and practices that promote safety, consent, and respect. By embracing the positive aspects of sex and addressing the challenges, we can create a better future for all.

CHAPTER 13

THE ART OF MAKING MONEY: A JOURNEY IN ENTREPRENEURSHIP

The journey of entrepreneurship is marked by highs and lows, successes and failures, and a constant quest for funding. It is not about having a perfect product but about raising funds with a minimum viable product (MVP) and mastering the skills of sales and persuasion. Through a narrative about a colleague's life, we will delve into the life of an entrepreneur who overcomes numerous challenges to achieve success by mastering the art of making money.

THE DREAM

Alex Carter always dreamed of creating something impactful. Growing up in a small town, Alex was fascinated by stories of entrepreneurs who built empires from scratch. After graduating from college with a degree in business, Alex moved to the bustling city of San Francisco, the heart of the tech world. With a mind full of ideas, Alex spent months brainstorming and sketching out plans for a groundbreaking app—an application designed to help users reduce their carbon footprint by making sustainable lifestyle choices. The concept was solid, but Alex knew that turning it into reality would require more than just an idea; it would require money.

The First Steps

Armed with a prototype, Alex began the journey of fundraising. The first step was to create a compelling pitch. The pitch needed to convey his vision, its potential impact, and why investors should believe in it. Alex spent countless hours refining the pitch, making sure it was clear, concise, and compelling. Next came networking. Alex attended every startup event, tech conference, and networking meetup possible. It was at one of these events that Alex met Jennifer, a seasoned entrepreneur and angel investor. Jennifer was intrigued by his vision and agreed to meet for coffee to discuss it further.

The First Pitch

Nervous but prepared, Alex met Jennifer at a cozy café. The pitch went smoothly, with Alex passionately explaining the vision behind his idea and its potential market. Jennifer listened intently, asking probing questions about the business model, target audience, and go-to-market strategy. Despite Alex's nerves, the passion and clarity of the vision shone through. Jennifer was impressed and decided to invest a small amount to help develop the MVP further. This initial investment was a crucial milestone, providing the validation and financial support Alex needed to move forward.

BUILDING THE MVP

With the initial funding secured, Alex hired a small team of developers and designers to build the MVP. The focus was on creating a functional, user-friendly app that demonstrated the core features. The development process was intense, filled with late nights and countless iterations. During this time, Alex also worked on building a community around his idea. By leveraging social media, blogs, and forums, Alex created a buzz and engaged with potential users to gather feedback and build anticipation for the app's launch.

The Art of Persuasion

As the MVP neared completion, Alex knew it was time to prepare for the next round of funding. This required mastering the art of persuasion. Alex studied successful pitches, learning how to craft a compelling narrative and present data in a way that resonated with investors. Key to this was understanding the psychology of investors. Alex learned to address their fears and concerns while highlighting the potential for high returns. By framing his vision as a solution to a significant problem with a growing market, Alex aimed to create a sense of urgency and opportunity.

THE SECOND ROUND

With the MVP ready, Alex set up meetings with several venture capitalists and angel investors. Each pitch was a learning experience, with Alex refining the presentation and addressing feedback. Some investors were skeptical, questioning the scalability and revenue model. Others were more optimistic but wanted to see more traction. Finally, Alex met with a top VC firm specializing in sustainable technology. The pitch went exceptionally well, with Alex confidently showcasing the MVP, user feedback, and growth projections. The VC firm saw the potential and offered a substantial investment, which Alex gratefully accepted.

Scaling Up

With the new funding, Alex scaled up operations. The team expanded, new features were added, and marketing efforts intensified. Alex focused on building partnerships with eco-friendly brands and organizations to enhance the app's value proposition. Sales became a critical focus. Alex hired a sales team and developed strategies to acquire users and monetize the app. By offering premium features and partnering with brands for exclusive discounts, the startup generated revenue and grew its user base.

Overcoming Challenges

Despite the progress, the journey was not without challenges. Technical issues, competition, and market shifts tested Alex's resilience. There were moments of doubt and frustration, but Alex remained committed to the vision. One significant setback occurred when a competitor launched a similar app with aggressive marketing. Growth stalled, and investors grew concerned. Alex knew that the key to overcoming this was differentiation and user loyalty. By listening to user feedback and continuously improving the app, the company regained its momentum.

The Power of Influence

As the startup grew, Alex realized that the true power of entrepreneurship lay in influencing decision-making. Whether it was convincing investors to fund the vision, persuading customers, or motivating the team to work tirelessly, influence was at the core of success. Alex honed the skills of storytelling, empathy, and negotiation. By understanding the motivations and concerns of different stakeholders, Alex was able to tailor messages and strategies to influence their decisions positively.

Diversifying Revenue Streams

To ensure long-term sustainability, Alex explored multiple revenue streams. In addition to premium subscriptions and brand partnerships, the app introduced a marketplace for eco-friendly products and services. This diversification not only increased revenue but also reinforced the company's mission of promoting sustainability. Alex also explored opportunities for corporate partnerships, offering a tool for companies to engage their employees in sustainability initiatives. This opened up a new market and provided additional revenue.

The Importance of Community

Throughout the journey, Alex recognized the importance of building a strong community. By fostering a sense of belonging and shared purpose, he created loyal users who became advocates for the app. Alex organized events, webinars, and online forums to engage with users and gather valuable feedback. This community-driven approach not only enhanced user retention but also attracted new users through word of mouth. By prioritizing the needs and experiences of the community, he built a strong brand and loyal customer base.

LESSONS LEARNED

Reflecting on the journey, Alex identified key lessons learned:

1. **Start with a Vision:** A clear and compelling vision is the foundation of any successful venture. It drives passion, attracts investors, and inspires the team.

2. **Master the MVP:** Building a functional MVP allows entrepreneurs to test their ideas, gather feedback, and demonstrate potential to investors.

3. **Influence and Persuasion:** Success in entrepreneurship hinges on the ability to influence and persuade others. This includes investors, customers, and team members.

4. **Resilience and Adaptability:** The journey is fraught with challenges. Resilience and adaptability are crucial for overcoming setbacks and seizing opportunities.

5. **Community and Feedback:** Building a strong community and actively seeking feedback enhances user loyalty and drives continuous improvement.

6. **Diversify Revenue Streams:** Exploring multiple revenue streams ensures long-term sustainability and mitigates risks.

THE HAPPY ENDING

Years later, Alex became a leader in the sustainable tech industry, impacting millions of lives and contributing to environmental conservation. Alex's journey from a dreamer with a prototype to a successful entrepreneur was a testament to the power of vision, influence, and resilience. As Alex stood on the stage at a major tech conference, sharing the story of his startup journey, it was clear that the art of making money was not just about financial success. It was about creating value, influencing positive change, and inspiring others to pursue their dreams.

The art of making money in entrepreneurship is a multifaceted journey. It requires a clear vision, the ability to build and present an MVP, and mastering the skills of influence and persuasion. It demands resilience, adaptability, and a commitment to continuous learning and improvement. The path to success is challenging, but with the right mindset and skills, it is possible to overcome obstacles and achieve the ultimate goal: making a positive impact while building a successful venture.

CHAPTER 14

MINTING MANIFESTATION: TURNING ENTREPRENEURIAL DREAMS INTO REALITY

In the entrepreneurial world, ideas are plentiful, but successful startups are few. Many dream of building the next big thing, but only a select few manage to turn those dreams into thriving businesses. The secret to their success often lies in their ability to manifest their ideas into reality. Manifestation isn't just about dreaming or wishful thinking—it's about transforming thoughts into concrete actions. Let's explore how entrepreneurs can harness the power of manifestation to bring their startup visions to life.

UNDERSTANDING MANIFESTATION

Manifestation is the process of bringing something into your life through belief, focus, and action. It involves visualizing your goals, maintaining a positive mindset, and taking deliberate steps to achieve them. For entrepreneurs, this means turning abstract ideas into tangible business ventures.

While manifestation might sound mystical, it has roots in psychology and neuroscience. The process engages the brain's reticular activating system (RAS), which filters information and focuses on what we deem important. By consistently focusing on your startup goals, you train your brain to recognize opportunities and resources that align with those goals.

The Steps to Manifesting Your Startup

1 CLARIFY YOUR VISION

Before you can manifest your startup, you need a clear and detailed vision. What does your startup look like? Who are your customers? What problem are you solving? The more specific you are, the easier it is to manifest.

Practical Exercise: Create a vision board that visually represents your startup goals. Include images, quotes, and keywords that resonate with your vision. Place your vision board where you'll see it daily to keep your goals top of mind.

2 SET SPECIFIC GOALS

General goals like "I want to start a business" are too vague. Set specific, measurable, achievable, relevant, and time-bound (SMART) goals. Instead of saying "I want to start a tech company," specify "By December 2024, I will launch a mobile app that helps users track their fitness goals.

Practical Exercise: Write down your goals using the SMART criteria. Break them down into smaller, actionable steps. For example, if your goal is to launch a mobile app, your steps might include market research, finding a developer, creating a prototype, and testing with users.

✿ DEVELOP A MANIFESTATION PLAN

A manifestation plan outlines the actions you'll take to achieve your goals. It includes strategies, timelines, and resources. Think of it as a business plan for your manifestation journey.

PRACTICAL EXERCISE Outline your business plan.

a. Executive Summary: brief overview of your startup vision and goals.

b. Market Analysis: research on your target market and competition.

c. Strategy: your approach to product development, marketing, and sales.

d. Timeline: key milestones and deadlines.

e. Resources: necessary resources, including funding, tools, and team members.

✿ VISUALIZE SUCCESS

Visualization is a powerful manifestation tool. Spend time each day visualizing your startup's success. Imagine your product being used by customers, receiving positive feedback, and achieving your financial goals.

Practical Exercise: Find a quiet space, close your eyes, and take deep breaths. Visualize your startup in vivid detail. Picture yourself working on your product, engaging with customers, and celebrating milestones. The more realistic and detailed your visualization, the more effective it will be.

🌸 TAKE ACTION

Manifestation requires action. Break down your goals into manageable tasks and tackle them one by one. Consistent, focused effort is key to turning your vision into reality.

PRACTICAL EXERCISE Create a daily action plan with specific tasks that move you closer to your goals. For example, if your goal is to secure funding, your daily tasks might include researching potential investors, preparing your pitch, and scheduling meeting.

🌸 MAINTAIN A POSITIVE MINDSET

A positive mindset is crucial for manifestation. Believe in your ability to succeed, even when faced with challenges. Surround yourself with positive influences, and practice gratitude for the progress you make.

PRACTICAL EXERCISE Keep a gratitude journal where you write down things you're thankful for each day. This helps maintain a positive outlook and keeps you focused on the positive aspects of your journey.

🌸 STAY PERSISTENT AND ADAPTABLE

Persistence is essential in the entrepreneurial journey. You'll face setbacks, but it's important to stay committed to your vision. Be adaptable and willing to adjust your plans as needed.

PRACTICAL EXERCISE View failures as learning opportunities. Analyze what went wrong, make necessary adjustments, and move forward with renewed determination. Successful entrepreneurs like Elon Musk and Sara Blakely have faced numerous setbacks but used them as stepping stones to success.

Real-World Examples of Manifestation in Action

EXAMPLE 1. STEVE JOBS AND APPLE

Steve Jobs had a clear vision for Apple: to create innovative products that would change the world. He maintained a relentless focus on this vision, setting specific goals and taking decisive actions. Jobs's belief in his vision, combined with his ability to take calculated risks and adapt to challenges, played a crucial role in Apple's success.

EXAMPLE 2. SARA BLAKELY AND SPANX

Sara Blakely, the founder of Spanx, is a prime example of manifestation in action. She started with a clear vision of creating comfortable and effective shapewear for women. Blakely set specific goals, such as securing a patent and getting her product into major retailers. Her unwavering belief in her vision and her ability to take consistent action helped her turn Spanx into a billion-dollar business.

EXAMPLE 3. ELON MUSK AND SpaceX

Elon Musk's vision for SpaceX was to reduce space transportation costs and enable the colonization of Mars. Despite facing numerous challenges and failures, Musk maintained a positive mindset and persisted in his efforts. He set specific goals, such as launching reusable rockets, and took decisive actions to achieve them. Musk's ability to manifest his vision has revolutionized the space industry.

Manifestation Techniques for Entrepreneurs

❶ AFFIRMATIONS

Affirmations are positive statements that reinforce your goals and beliefs. Repeat affirmations daily to build confidence and focus. For example, "I am capable of building a successful startup" or "My product will change lives."

❷ MEDITATION

Meditation helps clear your mind, reduce stress, and enhance focus. Incorporate meditation into your daily routine to improve mental clarity and creativity.

❸ VISION BOARDS

As mentioned earlier, vision boards are powerful tools for visualizing your goals. Update your vision board regularly to reflect your evolving vision and goals.

❹ NETWORKING

Surround yourself with like-minded individuals who support your vision. Attend industry events, join entrepreneurial groups, and seek mentorship from successful entrepreneurs.

❺ CONTINUOUS LEARNING

Stay informed and adaptable by continuously learning about your industry and improving your skills. Read books, attend workshops, and stay updated on market trends.

Practical Tips for Manifesting Your Startup

❶ START SMALL
Begin with small, achievable goals to build momentum. Celebrate each milestone to maintain motivation.

❷ STAY ORGANIZED
Keep track of your progress with tools like project management software, calendars, and to-do lists.

❸ SEEK FEEDBACK
Regularly seek feedback from customers, mentors, and peers to refine your product and strategy.

❹ STAY COMMITTED
Commit to your vision, even when faced with obstacles. Remember that setbacks are part of the journey and can provide valuable learning experiences.

❺ PRACTICE PATIENCE
Manifestation takes time. Be patient and trust the process, knowing that consistent effort will yield results.

Manifesting your startup is about more than just dreaming—it's about taking deliberate actions to turn your vision into reality. By clarifying your goals, developing a manifestation plan, visualizing success, and maintaining a positive mindset, you can overcome challenges and build a thriving business. Remember, the journey of manifestation is ongoing. Stay persistent, adaptable, and committed to your vision. By embracing the power of manifestation, you can transform your entrepreneurial dreams into tangible success, leaving a lasting impact on the world. So, dear entrepreneurs, it's time to harness the power of manifestation and take the first step toward building your dream startup. Your vision is within reach—believe in it, work for it, and watch it come to life.

CHAPTER 15

THE OBJECTIVE HEDONIST: MY PARISIAN REVELATION

In May 2023, I found myself in the heart of Paris. The City of Light had become the backdrop for a special occasion: a felicitation ceremony hosted by the French government in honor of my entrepreneurial achievements. This prestigious event celebrated my impact on the global tech industry, and the grandeur of the occasion was as inspiring as it was overwhelming. I had always been captivated by Paris's charm—its art, architecture, and, most importantly, its history of nurturing creativity and innovation. The ceremony was held at a historic venue, the Palais Garnier, where the opulence of the opera house added an extra layer of magic to the evening. As I mingled with esteemed guests and enjoyed the sumptuous dinner, I couldn't help but feel a sense of pride and excitement for the future.

Amidst the crowd of influential personalities, I was introduced to one of the high-ranking officials from the French government, Monsieur Étienne Dubois. A man in his early fifties with a dignified air and a sharp intellect, Dubois was known for his role in shaping France's economic policies and supporting innovation. The introduction was brief, but it set the stage for a memorable conversation that would profoundly influence my perspective on success and happiness.

As the evening progressed, I found myself seated next to

Dubois at a quiet corner table. The conversation began with pleasantries about the ceremony, but soon Dubois's interest shifted to my entrepreneurial journey. The discussion turned toward the philosophy of success and the personal satisfaction that comes with it. "Sharmin," Dubois began with a warm smile, "it's truly remarkable what you've achieved in such a short span. But tell me, how do you find personal fulfillment in your work?"

I hesitated, reflecting on my hectic schedule and constant drive for excellence. "I suppose I find fulfillment in the impact my work has on people's lives. Seeing my ideas come to life and make a difference is incredibly rewarding," I said. "But sometimes, it feels like there's always more to strive for."

Dubois nodded thoughtfully. "Ah, that's the essence of entre-preneurship—the relentless pursuit of improvement. Yet, there's a concept I'd like to share with you, something that might offer you a new perspective on finding balance and satisfaction. It's called objective hedonism."

My curiosity was piqued. "Objective hedonism? I'm not familiar with that term. Can you explain it to me?"

Dubois leaned in slightly, his eyes gleaming with enthusiasm. "Certainly. Objective hedonism is a philosophy that combines the pursuit of personal pleasure with a rational understanding of what constitutes true well-being," he explained. "Unlike sub-jective hedonism, which focuses solely on individual pleasure, objective hedonism takes into account universal principles of happiness and fulfillment. It's about aligning your actions with what genuinely brings you long-term satisfaction, while also considering broader values and goals."

I listened intently as Dubois continued, weaving his explana-tion with practical examples and philosophical insights.

UNDERSTANDING OBJECTIVE HEDONISM

❶ Pursuing True Pleasure over Transient Joy

Dubois began by illustrating the core of objective hedonism: the distinction between transient pleasure and true, enduring satisfaction. "Consider a successful entrepreneur," he said. "In the short term, attending lavish parties or acquiring luxury items might provide immediate gratification. However, these are fleeting pleasures. Objective hedonism emphasizes seeking pleasure that aligns with deeper values and contributes to long-term well-being." He shared an example of a renowned chef he once knew. "This chef found immense joy not just in the act of cooking but in the way his culinary creations brought people together and created memorable experiences. His true pleasure came from the impact he made rather than the accolades or material rewards."

I nodded, recognizing the truth in Dubois's words. "I can relate to that. The moments when I see my team thrive or when our technology solves a real problem are far more satisfying than any external validation."

❷ Balancing Personal Fulfillment with Societal Contribution

Dubois continued, "Another aspect of objective hedonism is the balance between personal fulfillment and contributing to the greater good. True happiness often involves aligning your personal goals with positive impacts on others." He recounted the story of a social entrepreneur who created a sustainable fashion brand. "This entrepreneur was passionate about fashion, but she also wanted to address environmental issues. By integrating sustainability into her business model, she not only pursued her passion but also contributed to a cause she cared about deeply. Her success came from balancing personal joy with societal benefits."

I reflected on my own journey and the ways my startup aimed to address societal challenges. "It's reassuring to know that the impact we aim to make can also enhance our own sense of fulfillment," I said.

❸ Embracing Challenges as Part of the Journey

Dubois emphasized that objective hedonism also involves embracing challenges and difficulties as part of the journey toward fulfillment. "Entrepreneurship is inherently challenging. The key is to view these challenges as opportunities for growth and learning rather than obstacles to happiness." He shared the story of a technology startup that faced numerous setbacks but persisted through innovation and resilience. "The founders didn't see the challenges as barriers but as integral to their growth. Their eventual success was a result of their ability to find joy and purpose in overcoming difficulties."

I considered how the challenges I had faced—such as market fluctuations and team dynamics—had contributed to my personal growth and the growth of my company. "It's encouraging to see that difficulties can be reframed as part of the journey toward achieving long-term satisfaction."

APPLYING OBJECTIVE HEDONISM TO ENTREPRENEURSHIP

❶ Aligning Business Goals with Personal Values

Dubois advised me to align my business goals with my personal values and passions. "When your work reflects what you genuinely care about, it not only brings personal satisfaction but also creates a sense of purpose that resonates with others." He suggested conducting a personal values assessment and comparing it with my company's mission. "Ensure that your startup's objectives align with your core values. This alignment will not only enhance your fulfillment but also attract like-minded individuals to your team and your customers."

I made a mental note to revisit my company's mission statement and ensure that it reflected my personal values and vision.

❷ Focusing on Long-Term Impact

Dubois encouraged me to focus on the long-term impact of my work rather than immediate rewards. "Investing in initiatives that have a lasting positive effect can provide deeper satisfaction than short-term gains." He cited the example of a tech entrepreneur who invested in educational programs for underserved communities. "The long-term impact of these programs created lasting change and brought the entrepreneur a profound sense of fulfillment, far beyond immediate business success."

I realized that focusing on the broader impact of my work could lead to more enduring satisfaction.

❸ Practicing Gratitude and Reflection

To cultivate a mindset of objective hedonism, Dubois suggested incorporating gratitude and reflection into my routine. "Regularly reflecting on your achievements and expressing gratitude for the opportunities and support you have can enhance your sense of fulfillment." He recommended setting aside time each week for reflection and gratitude practices. "This habit can help you stay grounded and appreciative of your journey, even amidst the challenges."

I agreed to implement these practices into my routine to foster a more balanced perspective.

THE DINNER'S CONCLUSION

As the evening drew to a close, I felt a renewed sense of purpose and clarity. Dubois's insights on objective hedonism had provided me with a fresh perspective on balancing personal satisfaction with broader goals. The conversation had not only been intellectually stimulating but had also offered practical guidance for navigating the entrepreneurial landscape. As we said our goodbyes, Dubois offered me a final piece of advice. "Remember, Sharmin, the path of entrepreneurship is filled with both triumphs and trials. Embrace the journey with a mindset of objective hedonism, and you will find that true fulfillment comes from aligning your passion with meaningful impact."

I thanked Dubois for his wisdom and inspiration. "Your insights have given me a new perspective on how to approach my work and find deeper satisfaction. I appreciate the opportunity to learn from you."

As I left the Palais Garnier, I felt a sense of excitement and determination. The ideas of objective hedonism resonated deeply with me, and I was eager to apply them to my entrepreneurial journey. Paris had not only been a city of celebration but had also become a place of profound personal growth. The night sky was clear, and the lights of Paris shimmered in the distance as I walked back to my hotel. The city of Paris, with its rich history and cultural vibrancy, had offered me more than just accolades—it had provided me with a transformative lesson in finding joy and fulfillment amidst the chaos of entrepreneurship. As I reflected on my conversation with Dubois, I knew that my journey ahead would be marked by a deeper understanding of what it meant to achieve true fulfillment in life.

CHAPTER 16

AS YOU LIKE IT: LESSONS FOR ENTREPRENEURS FROM SHAKESPEARE'S STAGE

INTRODUCTION: THE STAGE OF ENTREPRENEURSHIP

William Shakespeare's play *As You Like It* opens with one of the most famous lines in literature: "All the world's a stage, and all the men and women merely players." This metaphorical declaration encapsulates the idea that life is a performance, and each person has a role to play. For entrepreneurs, this analogy offers profound insights into their journey. In the realm of entrepreneurship, the stage represents the business world—a dynamic, ever-changing environment where every individual plays a part. Entrepreneurs, as the central characters, must navigate this stage with skill, adaptability, and creativity. Understanding this metaphor can provide valuable lessons on how to approach business challenges, manage relationships, and craft a meaningful narrative.

ACT I: THE WORLD'S A STAGE— THE ENTREPRENEURIAL ROLE

Understanding the Metaphor

In *As You Like It*, Shakespeare uses the stage metaphor to explore the roles and personas individuals assume throughout their lives. Similarly, in entrepreneurship, recognizing that the business world is a stage can help entrepreneurs understand their roles and responsibilities. Entrepreneurs are often cast in various roles: leader, innovator, negotiator, and problem-solver. Each role requires a different set of skills and perspectives. By embracing these roles and understanding their importance, entrepreneurs can navigate their business journey more effectively.

Embracing Your Role in the Startup Ecosystem

The startup ecosystem is a complex stage with numerous players—investors, customers, competitors, and collaborators. Entrepreneurs must identify their role within this ecosystem and play it to the best of their ability. This involves understanding market needs, building a strong team, and continuously adapting to changes. Just as actors rehearse and perfect their roles, entrepreneurs must refine their skills and strategies. This preparation and adaptation are crucial for succeeding in a competitive environment.

ACT II: THE SEVEN AGES OF THE ENTREPRENEUR

Childhood: The Spark of Innovation

The entrepreneurial journey often begins with a spark of innovation—a new idea or a vision for solving a problem. This phase is characterized by excitement and exploration, much like the youthful enthusiasm described in Shakespeare's play. Entrepreneurs in this stage are driven by passion and curiosity. They are eager to experiment and learn. Embracing this phase with an open mind and a willingness to take risks is essential for laying a strong foundation for future success.

Adolescence: The Trials of Learning

As entrepreneurs transition into the adolescent stage, they encounter challenges and setbacks. This phase is marked by learning and growth. Just as the characters in *As You Like It* face trials and tribulations, entrepreneurs must navigate obstacles and refine their strategies. Resilience and perseverance are key traits during this stage. Entrepreneurs should view challenges as opportunities for growth and learning. This mindset will help them overcome difficulties and build a more robust business.

Adulthood: The Height of Ambition

The adulthood stage represents the peak of ambition and achievement. Entrepreneurs in this phase are focused on scaling their business, reaching new markets, and achieving their goals. This stage requires strategic planning, leadership, and a clear vision. Shakespeare's depiction of adulthood in *As You Like It* highlights the complexities of this phase. Entrepreneurs must balance ambition with practicality and continue to innovate while managing growth.

Old Age: The Wisdom of Experience

The final stage, old age, is characterized by wisdom and reflection. Entrepreneurs who reach this stage have accumulated valuable experience and insights. They can use this knowledge to mentor others, guide their business through transitions, and reflect on their legacy. This stage involves looking back on the journey and evaluating what has been achieved. Entrepreneurs should embrace this phase with a sense of accomplishment and a commitment to leaving a positive impact on their industry and community.

ACT III: THE FOREST OF ARDEN— A REALM OF OPPORTUNITIES

The Significance of the Forest

In *As You Like It*, the Forest of Arden symbolizes a place of refuge and transformation. It is where characters escape from the constraints of court life and discover new aspects of themselves. For entrepreneurs, the Forest of Arden represents a realm of opportunities and innovation. The entrepreneurial journey often involves venturing into uncharted territory, much like entering the forest. This stage offers a chance to experiment, innovate, and explore new possibilities. Embracing the unknown and adapting to change are crucial for discovering new opportunities and achieving success.

Embracing Uncertainty and Innovation

The forest is a metaphor for the uncertainty and unpredictability that entrepreneurs face. Embracing this uncertainty can lead to innovative solutions and creative breakthroughs. Entrepreneurs should view challenges as opportunities for growth and be open to exploring new ideas and approaches. By navigating the forest with curiosity and resilience, entrepreneurs can uncover hidden potential and drive their ventures forward. This mindset of exploration and adaptability is essential for thriving in a dynamic business environment.

ACT IV: THE PLAY WITHIN THE PLAY— AUTHENTICITY AND BRANDING

The Role of Authenticity in Entrepreneurship

In *As You Like It*, the play within the play serves as a commentary on authenticity and self-expression. For entrepreneurs, authenticity is crucial for building trust and credibility with customers, investors, and team members. Authenticity involves staying true to your values, vision, and mission. It means presenting yourself and your business in a genuine and transparent manner. This approach helps build strong relationships and fosters a positive brand reputation.

Crafting Your Brand Narrative

Just as characters in *As You Like It* perform their roles, entrepreneurs must craft a compelling brand narrative. This narrative should reflect the core values and unique aspects of the business. A well-crafted narrative helps differentiate your brand and connect with your audience on a deeper level. Entrepreneurs should focus on creating a story that resonates with their target market and highlights the value they bring. This narrative should be woven into all aspects of the business, from marketing materials to customer interactions.

ACT V: LOVE AND RELATIONSHIPS— BUILDING AND LEADING TEAMS

The Dynamics of Relationships in Business

As You Like It explores various forms of love and relationships, emphasizing the importance of human connections. In entrepreneurship, building and leading a strong team is essential for success. The dynamics of relationships play a crucial role in fostering collaboration, trust, and productivity. Entrepreneurs must focus on cultivating positive relationships with their team members, partners, and stakeholders. This involves effective communication, empathy, and support. By creating a collaborative and supportive environment, entrepreneurs can enhance team performance and drive business success.

Leadership Lessons from *As You Like It*

Shakespeare's play offers valuable insights into leadership and team dynamics. The characters in *As You Like It* demonstrate different leadership styles and approaches. Entrepreneurs can draw lessons from these characters to develop their leadership skills and create a positive work culture. Effective leadership involves inspiring and motivating others, providing clear direction, and fostering a sense of purpose. Entrepreneurs should strive to be approachable, supportive, and visionary leaders who empower their teams to achieve their best.

ACT VI: THE POWER OF HUMOR AND RESILIENCE

The Role of Humor in Overcoming Challenges

Humor plays a significant role in *As You Like It*, providing relief and perspective in the midst of challenges. For entrepreneurs, humor can be a powerful tool for managing stress, building relationships, and maintaining a positive outlook. Embracing humor and a light-hearted approach can help entrepreneurs navigate the ups and downs of their journey. It can also foster a positive work environment and strengthen team cohesion. Entrepreneurs should find ways to incorporate humor into their daily routines and interactions.

Resilience and Adaptability in Business

Resilience and adaptability are essential traits for entrepreneurs. The ability to bounce back from setbacks, adapt to changing circumstances, and maintain a positive attitude is crucial for long-term success. Shakespeare's characters in *As You Like It* exhibit resilience and adaptability as they navigate their challenges and transformations. Entrepreneurs can draw inspiration from these characters and apply the same principles to their own ventures.

ACT VII: REFLECTION AND LEGACY

Reflecting on Your Entrepreneurial Journey

Reflection is an important aspect of the entrepreneurial journey. Just as characters in *As You Like It* reflect on their experiences and relationships, entrepreneurs should take time to evaluate their progress, achievements, and challenges. Regular reflection helps entrepreneurs gain insights into their strengths and areas for improvement. It also provides an opportunity to celebrate successes and learn from failures. Entrepreneurs should incorporate reflection into their routine and use it to guide their future decisions.

Building a Legacy

Building a legacy involves creating a meaningful impact and leaving a positive mark on the world. Entrepreneurs should focus on contributing to their industry, community, and society in a way that aligns with their values and vision. A legacy is built through ethical leadership, innovation, and a commitment to social responsibility. Entrepreneurs should strive to create value and make a difference, ensuring that their impact extends beyond their business.

CONCLUSION: TAKING THE STAGE

William Shakespeare's *As You Like It* offers valuable lessons and insights for entrepreneurs. The metaphor of life as a stage provides a powerful framework for understanding the entrepreneurial journey. By embracing their roles, navigating challenges, building relationships, and reflecting on their journey, entrepreneurs can achieve success and create a lasting impact.

The lessons from *As You Like It*—resilience, adaptability, authenticity, and ethical leadership—are essential for navigating the complex and dynamic world of entrepreneurship. By applying these principles, entrepreneurs can take the stage with confidence, creativity, and a commitment to making a positive difference. As you embark on your entrepreneurial journey, remember that all the world's a stage, and you have the power to shape your performance. Embrace your role, stay true to your values, and strive to leave a legacy that inspires and uplifts others. The stage is yours—take it with purpose and passion.

CHAPTER 17

MEN BUILD TOO MANY WALLS AND NOT ENOUGH BRIDGES

I sat in my small, cluttered office, staring at my computer screen. The startup I had poured my heart and soul into for the prior three years was struggling. The numbers were grim, and my team was feeling the pressure. It wasn't the technology or the business model that was failing; it was something more profound, something I couldn't quite put my finger on. I had always prided myself on my analytical skills and strategic thinking. I had worked at a very successful startup before deciding to launch my own venture. But now, faced with the harsh reality of potential failure, I realized that there was a crucial element missing from my approach. One evening, as I browsed through my social media feed, I stumbled upon a quote: "Men build too many walls and not enough bridges." The words struck a chord with me. I realized that in my pursuit of success, I had focused too much on the barriers and challenges and not enough on building connections and fostering empathy within my team and with my customers.

THE WALLS WE BUILD

I reflected on the walls I had built. I had always believed in maintaining a strict professional distance with my team. I thought this approach would help me maintain authority and control. However, it had created an atmosphere of fear and isolation. My team members were reluctant to share their ideas or concerns, and this lack of open communication was stifling innovation. I also recognized that I had built walls between my startup and its customers. The company's marketing campaigns were polished and professional, but they lacked a personal touch. Customers didn't feel a connection to the brand, and as a result, loyalty was hard to come by.

Determined to change, I decided to start with my team. I called for a meeting—not in the usual conference room but in a cozy, informal setting. I began by sharing my own struggles and vulnerabilities, something I had never done before. I encouraged my team to do the same. It was awkward at first, but gradually, people started opening up. They shared their fears, their frustrations, and their dreams for the company.

BUILDING BRIDGES

As the walls began to crumble, something beautiful happened. The team began to bond on a deeper level. They started collaborating more freely, and new ideas flowed. I noticed a significant improvement in morale and productivity. I realized that by showing empathy and vulnerability, I had created a bridge that connected me with my team on a human level. Inspired by this change, I decided to apply the same principles to my interactions with customers. I organized a series of focus groups and community events, where my team and I could meet customers face-to-face.

We listened to their stories, understood their needs, and shared the company's vision in a more personal way.

One of the customers, a small business owner named Chetan, shared his struggles with acquiring more customers. He explained how good quality content could disrupt his entire operation, and tracking the performance of this content would be a game changer. I listened intently, empathizing with his challenges. I realized that my company's software could be modified to help small business owners like Chetan by providing real-time performance tracking and alerts.

The Power of Empathy

The changes I implemented had a profound impact on the company. Sales began to increase as customers felt more connected to the brand. The product improvements based on customer feedback made the software more valuable and user-friendly. The company started receiving positive reviews and referrals, which further boosted its growth. My journey was not without its challenges. There were moments of doubt and setbacks along the way. However, I remained committed to building bridges instead of walls. I continued to foster a culture of empathy within my team and with my customers.

One evening, after a particularly long day, I received an email from Chetan. He thanked me for listening to his concerns and for making the changes to the software. He shared how the new features had significantly improved his business operations. He wrote, "Your willingness to understand my challenges and act on them has made a real difference in my life. Thank you for building that bridge."

The Broader Impact

My approach began to catch the attention of the broader business community. I was invited to speak at industry conferences and share my experiences. I used these platforms to advocate for empathy in entrepreneurship, emphasizing that success wasn't just about financial metrics but also about human connections. At one of these conferences, I met Dr. Emily Carter, a renowned psychologist who had researched the impact of empathy in leadership. Dr. Carter explained that empathy was a critical component of emotional intelligence, which was strongly correlated with effective leadership and business success. She shared examples from her research, demonstrating how empathetic leaders could inspire loyalty, foster innovation, and create a positive organizational culture. Dr. Carter and I decided to collaborate on a workshop series for entrepreneurs, teaching them how to cultivate empathy in their leadership style. The workshops were well-received, and participants reported significant improvements in their team dynamics and customer relationships.

Empathy as a Business Strategy

As I continued to integrate empathy into my business strategy, I saw its ripple effects throughout the organization. The company's retention rates improved as employees felt more valued and connected. Customer satisfaction and loyalty increased, leading to more stable and predictable revenue streams. One particular success story stood out. Rashmi, a talented software engineer on my team, had been struggling with burnout and had considered leaving the company. After the shift in company culture, where empathy and open communication were prioritized, Rashmi felt more supported. She decided to stay and eventually led the development of a groundbreaking feature that set the company apart from its competitors.

My commitment to empathy also led to innovative partnerships. I collaborated with other startups and organizations that shared similar values. These partnerships resulted in joint ventures and co-branded products that expanded the company's reach and impact.

Challenges and Growth

Despite the positive changes, I faced resistance from some stakeholders who were skeptical of my emphasis on empathy. Some investors questioned whether this "soft" approach could yield tangible results. I remained steadfast, providing data and examples of how empathy-driven strategies had improved the company's performance. Over time, the results spoke for themselves. The company's growth rate accelerated, and its reputation as a customer-centric and employee-friendly organization attracted top talent and loyal customers. Investors who had once been doubtful became staunch supporters.

My journey also had a personal dimension. The relationships I built with my team and customers enriched my life in unexpected ways. I formed genuine friendships and found joy in helping others succeed. This sense of fulfillment became a powerful motivator, driving me to continue building bridges and breaking down walls.

A LEGACY OF EMPATHY

As I look back on my entrepreneurial journey, I feel a deep sense of gratitude. I had not only built a successful business but also created a positive and lasting impact on the lives of many people. The company's culture of empathy had become its defining characteristic, shaping its identity and guiding its decisions.

My story continues to unfold as I explore new ways to integrate empathy into my business and personal life. I have become a keynote speaker, sharing my insights at conferences and events around the world. One of my most memorable speeches was at my alma mater, where I addressed a group of aspiring entrepreneurs. I spoke passionately about the importance of empathy, urging them to build bridges and create meaningful connections. I reminded them that success was not just about financial achievements but also about making a positive impact on the world. As I stepped off the stage, I felt a sense of fulfillment and purpose. I had come a long way from the days of building walls and facing isolation. By embracing empathy, entrepreneurs can build bridges that connect, inspire, and transform.

CHAPTER 18

CREATING LEADERS THROUGH SMART AUTHORITY DELEGATION

*When you delegate tasks, you create
followers. When you delegate authority,
you create leaders.*

—CRAIG GROESCHEL, FOUNDER OF LIFE CHURCH

Delegation is more than just assigning tasks to others; it is about entrusting others with the responsibility and authority to make decisions and take ownership. For entrepreneurs, the act of delegation is crucial for the growth and success of their startup. However, many entrepreneurs struggle with this concept, often feeling the need to control every aspect of their business. "When you delegate tasks, you create followers. When you delegate authority, you create leaders." The quote encapsulates the essence of effective delegation. Let's explore the importance of delegation in entrepreneurship and discuss practical insights on how to delegate tasks and authority smartly to foster leadership within the organization.

Delegation is the process of transferring responsibility and authority from one person to another. In the context of entrepreneurship, it involves assigning tasks and decision-making power to team members. Effective delegation empowers employees, fosters a sense of ownership, and promotes leadership development.

THE IMPORTANCE OF DELEGATION IN ENTREPRENEURSHIP

For entrepreneurs, delegation is essential for several reasons:

1. Scalability: As a startup grows, the founder cannot manage every aspect of the business. Delegation allows for scalability by distributing responsibilities across the team.

2. Focus on Core Activities: Delegating routine tasks frees up the entrepreneur's time to focus on strategic and core activities that drive the business forward.

3. Employee Development: Delegation helps in developing employees' skills and confidence, preparing them for leadership roles.

4. Innovation: By delegating tasks and authority, entrepreneurs can encourage creativity and innovation within the team.

COMMON MISCONCEPTIONS ABOUT DELEGATION

Many entrepreneurs have misconceptions about delegation, such as the following:

1. Loss of Control: fear of losing control over the business.

2. Time Concerns: belief that delegation takes more time than doing tasks themselves.

3. Quality Concerns: worry that others may not perform tasks to their standards.

Addressing these misconceptions is the first step toward effective delegation.

THE BENEFITS OF DELEGATION

❶ Empowering Employees

When entrepreneurs delegate authority, they empower their employees to make decisions and take ownership of their work. This empowerment leads to higher job satisfaction, increased motivation, and a stronger sense of responsibility.

❷ Fostering Leadership

Delegating authority helps in identifying and nurturing potential leaders within the organization. It allows employees to develop their leadership skills and prepares them for future leadership roles.

❸ Enhancing Productivity

Delegation improves overall productivity by ensuring that tasks are handled by the most qualified individuals. It allows the entrepreneur to focus on high-priority tasks while others handle routine or specialized tasks.

❹ Encouraging Innovation

When employees are given the authority to make decisions, they are more likely to come up with innovative solutions. Delegation fosters a culture of creativity and continuous improvement.

⑤ Reducing Burnout

For entrepreneurs, trying to do everything themselves can lead to burnout. Delegation helps in distributing the workload, reducing stress, and preventing burnout.

THE PRINCIPLES OF EFFECTIVE DELEGATION

① Trust and Accountability

Trust is the foundation of effective delegation. Entrepreneurs must trust their team members and hold them accountable for their responsibilities. This trust encourages employees to take ownership and perform to the best of their abilities.

② Clear Communication

Clear and effective communication is crucial for delegation. Entrepreneurs must clearly define tasks, expectations, and deadlines. Open communication channels ensure that employees can seek clarification and provide updates on their progress.

③ Matching Skills and Tasks

Delegating tasks based on employees' skills and strengths is essential for success. Entrepreneurs should assess their team's capabilities and assign tasks accordingly. This alignment ensures that tasks are completed efficiently and effectively.

④ Providing Resources and Support

Delegation involves not only assigning tasks but also providing the necessary resources and support. Entrepreneurs should ensure that their team members have access to the tools, information, and guidance needed to complete their tasks successfully.

5 Monitoring and Feedback

While delegation involves trusting employees with tasks and authority, it is also important to monitor their progress and provide constructive feedback. Regular check-ins and feedback sessions help in identifying any issues and ensuring that tasks are on track.

STEPS TO EFFECTIVE DELEGATION

1 Identify Tasks to Delegate

The first step in effective delegation is identifying tasks that can be delegated. Entrepreneurs should make a list of all their tasks and responsibilities and determine which ones can be handled by others. Routine and repetitive tasks, tasks that require specialized skills, and tasks that can be handled by others without compromising quality should be considered for delegation.

2 Assess Team Members' Skills

Entrepreneurs should assess their team members' skills, strengths, and interests. This assessment helps in matching tasks to the most suitable individuals. Understanding employees' capabilities ensures that tasks are delegated to those who are best equipped to handle them.

3 Define Clear Objectives and Expectations

Before delegating a task, it is important to define clear objectives and expectations. Entrepreneurs should clearly communicate the task's purpose, desired outcomes, deadlines, and any specific guidelines. Clear objectives and expectations provide a roadmap for employees and ensure that they understand what is required of them.

❹ Provide Training and Resources

Providing the necessary training and resources is crucial for effective delegation. Entrepreneurs should ensure that their team members have access to the tools, information, and support needed to complete their tasks successfully. Providing training and resources helps in building employees' confidence and competence.

❺ Delegate Authority

Delegating authority involves giving employees the power to make decisions related to their tasks. Entrepreneurs should empower their team members by delegating not just tasks but also the authority to make decisions. This empowerment fosters a sense of ownership and responsibility.

❻ Monitor Progress and Provide Feedback

While it is important to trust employees with delegated tasks, monitoring progress and providing feedback is equally important. Regular check-ins and feedback sessions help in identifying any issues and ensuring that tasks are on track. Constructive feedback helps in improving performance and achieving desired outcomes.

❼ Recognize and Reward Efforts

Recognizing and rewarding employees' efforts is crucial for fostering a positive work environment. Entrepreneurs should acknowledge and appreciate their team members' contributions. Recognition and rewards motivate employees and encourage them to take ownership and perform to the best of their abilities.

OVERCOMING DELEGATION CHALLENGES

❶ Letting Go of Control

One of the biggest challenges entrepreneurs face in delegation is letting go of control. Many entrepreneurs struggle with the fear of losing control over their business. To overcome this challenge, entrepreneurs should focus on building trust with their team members and empowering them with the necessary authority and resources.

❷ Building Trust

Building trust is essential for effective delegation. Entrepreneurs should foster a culture of trust by being transparent, communicating openly, and demonstrating trust in their team members. Trust is built over time through consistent actions and positive interactions.

❸ Addressing Quality Concerns

Entrepreneurs often worry that others may not perform tasks to their standards. To address quality concerns, entrepreneurs should provide clear instructions, set expectations, and offer support and guidance. Regular monitoring and feedback help in maintaining quality and achieving desired outcomes.

❹ Managing Resistance

Resistance to delegation can come from both entrepreneurs and employees. Entrepreneurs may be reluctant to delegate tasks, while employees may be hesitant to take on additional responsibilities. To manage resistance, entrepreneurs should communicate the benefits of delegation, provide support, and create a positive and inclusive work environment.

❺ Ensuring Accountability

Ensuring accountability is crucial for successful delegation. Entrepreneurs should clearly define responsibilities, set expectations, and establish accountability mechanisms. Regular check-ins and feedback sessions help in holding employees accountable for their tasks and ensuring that they meet their objectives.

CASE STUDIES: SUCCESSFUL DELEGATION IN ENTREPRENEURSHIP

CASE STUDY 1. Google

Google is a prime example of a company that has successfully implemented delegation. The company's founders, Larry Page and Sergey Brin, recognized the importance of delegating authority and empowering employees. Google's organizational structure encourages innovation and creativity by allowing employees to take ownership of their projects and make decisions. This approach has led to groundbreaking products and services, making Google one of the most successful companies in the world.

CASE STUDY 2. Apple

Steve Jobs, cofounder of Apple, was known for his visionary leadership. However, he also understood the importance of delegation. Jobs surrounded himself with talented individuals and trusted them with significant responsibilities. He delegated authority to key executives, allowing them to make decisions and drive innovation. This approach enabled Apple to develop iconic products and achieve unparalleled success.

CASE STUDY 3: Amazon

Jeff Bezos, the founder of Amazon, built the company on the principles of delegation and empowerment. Bezos believed in hiring the best talent and giving them the autonomy to make decisions. Amazon's decentralized structure allows teams to operate independently and innovate rapidly. This approach has made Amazon a leader in e-commerce and technology.

CASE STUDY 4: Airbnb

Airbnb's founders, Brian Chesky, Joe Gebbia, and Nathan Blecharczyk, understood the importance of delegation in scaling their business. They delegated authority to regional managers and allowed them to make decisions based on local market conditions. This decentralized approach enabled Airbnb to expand globally and become a dominant player in the hospitality industry.

CASE STUDY 5: Tesla

Elon Musk, the CEO of Tesla, is known for his hands-on leadership style. However, he also recognizes the importance of delegation. Musk delegates authority to key executives and trusts them to make decisions. This approach has allowed Tesla to innovate and disrupt the automotive industry.

DELEGATION AND LEADERSHIP DEVELOPMENT

Delegation plays a crucial role in leadership development. By delegating authority, entrepreneurs provide their team members with opportunities to develop their leadership skills. Delegation helps in identifying potential leaders and preparing them for future leadership roles. Let's explore some key components for leadership development through delegation.

Developing a Leadership Pipeline

Entrepreneurs should focus on developing a leadership pipeline within their organization. This involves identifying and nurturing potential leaders, providing them with opportunities for growth, and preparing them for leadership roles. Delegation is a key component of developing a leadership pipeline.

Empowering Employees to Lead

Empowering employees to lead involves giving them the authority to make decisions and take ownership of their tasks. Entrepreneurs should create a culture of empowerment by delegating authority, providing support, and recognizing and rewarding leadership efforts.

Encouraging Initiative and Innovation

Delegation encourages initiative and innovation by allowing employees to take ownership of their tasks and make decisions. Entrepreneurs should foster a culture of innovation by delegating authority, providing resources, and encouraging employees to think creatively.

Providing Opportunities for Growth

Delegation provides employees with opportunities for growth and development. Entrepreneurs should identify and delegate tasks that challenge employees and help them develop their skills. Providing opportunities for growth helps in building a strong and capable leadership team.

DELEGATION IN DIFFERENT STAGES OF A STARTUP

Delegation in the Early Stages

In the early stages of a startup, entrepreneurs often wear multiple hats and handle a wide range of tasks. However, as the business grows, it becomes essential to delegate tasks to ensure scalability and focus on core activities. Entrepreneurs should start by delegating routine and specialized tasks to their team members.

Delegation in the Growth Stage

During the growth stage, the startup expands and the workload increases. Entrepreneurs should focus on delegating authority and empowering their team members to make decisions. Delegating authority helps in managing the increased workload and encourages leadership development.

Delegation in the Maturity Stage

In the maturity stage, the startup has a stable and established structure. Entrepreneurs should focus on delegating strategic responsibilities and developing a strong leadership team. Delegating strategic responsibilities helps in driving innovation and ensuring long-term success.

Delegation in the Scaling Stage

During the scaling stage, the startup expands rapidly and enters new markets. Entrepreneurs should delegate authority to regional and functional leaders to manage the expansion. Delegating authority ensures that decisions are made based on local market conditions and helps in managing the complexities of scaling.

Delegation in the Exit Stage

An entrepreneur may plan to exit the business through acquisition or IPO. Delegating authority and developing a strong leadership team is crucial for ensuring a smooth transition during the exit stage. Entrepreneurs should focus on building a capable leadership team that can manage the business independently.

TOOLS FOR EFFECTIVE DELEGATION

Task Management Tools

Task management tools help in organizing and tracking tasks and responsibilities. Tools like Trello, Asana, and Monday.com provide a visual interface for managing tasks, setting deadlines, and tracking progress. These tools facilitate effective delegation by providing clarity and transparency.

Communication Tools

Effective communication is crucial for delegation. Communication tools like Slack, Microsoft Teams, and Zoom facilitate real-time communication and collaboration. These tools ensure that team members can seek clarification, provide updates, and collaborate effectively.

Project Management Tools

Project management tools like Basecamp, Jira, and Wrike help in managing complex projects and delegating tasks. These tools provide a comprehensive platform for planning, executing, and tracking projects. They facilitate effective delegation by providing a structured approach to project management.

Performance Management Tools

Performance management tools like 15Five, Lattice, and BambooHR help in tracking employee performance and providing feedback. These tools facilitate effective delegation by ensuring that employees are held accountable for their tasks and receive constructive feedback.

Collaboration Tools

Collaboration tools like Google Workspace, Microsoft 365, and Dropbox facilitate collaboration and file sharing. These tools ensure that team members can collaborate effectively and have access to the resources they need to complete their tasks.

Delegation is a critical skill for entrepreneurs. It involves not just assigning tasks but also empowering employees with the authority to make decisions and take ownership. Effective delegation creates a positive and supportive work environment, fosters leadership development, and drives business success. Entrepreneurs should focus on building trust, communicating clearly, providing support, and recognizing efforts. By delegating tasks and authority smartly, entrepreneurs can create a capable and motivated team that drives the business forward.

The journey of entrepreneurship is not just about achieving financial success but also about creating a positive impact on the lives of others. By embracing delegation, entrepreneurs can build a strong and capable leadership team that contributes to the long-term success and sustainability of the business. Delegation is not just a management technique but a leadership philosophy. It is about building bridges, fostering trust, and creating leaders. Entrepreneurs who master the art of delegation can achieve remarkable success and leave a legacy.

CHAPTER 19

BREAKING FREE FROM THE NINE-TO-FIVE: EMBRACE ENTREPRENEURSHIP AND TRANSFORM YOUR LIFE

The nine-to-five job: a symbol of stability, a steady paycheck, and a predictable routine. For many, it represents the comfort and security of knowing what each day will bring. Yet for countless others, it becomes a symbol of monotony, a reminder of untapped potential, and a barrier to true fulfillment. If you're reading this, chances are you've felt the stirrings of dissatisfaction, the urge to break free from the daily grind, and the desire to carve out a path of your own. The journey from employee to entrepreneur is not just a career shift; it's a profound transformation of mindset, lifestyle, and purpose. It's about daring to dream, embracing the unknown, and having the courage to pursue a life that aligns with your passions and ambitions.

THE COMFORT ZONE CONUNDRUM

The comfort zone is a psychological state where things feel familiar, where we feel in control, and where minimal stress and risk are involved. It's a space where we operate on autopilot, performing tasks we're accustomed to without much conscious effort. While the comfort zone offers a sense of safety and predictability, it also imposes significant limitations on our personal and professional growth.

The Perils of Staying Comfortable

Staying within the confines of the comfort zone can lead to a stagnant lifestyle. Over time, the routine of a nine-to-five job can become monotonous, sapping your energy and enthusiasm. The security of a steady paycheck can become a golden handcuff, preventing you from exploring new opportunities and realizing your true potential.

Signs You're Stuck in a Rut

1. Lack of Passion: You wake up each morning with a sense of dread or indifference toward your job.

2. Routine Overload: Every day feels the same, with little variation or excitement.

3. Limited Growth: You're not learning new skills or facing new challenges.

4. Financial Stagnation: Despite working hard, you're living paycheck to paycheck with little to no savings.

5. Unfulfilled Dreams: You have aspirations and ideas that you've never pursued.

THE ENTREPRENEURIAL MINDSET

Embracing the Unknown

Entrepreneurship is inherently about venturing into the unknown. It's about seeing possibilities where others see obstacles and having the faith to pursue your vision even when the path isn't clear. This requires a shift in mindset from one of security and predictability to one of curiosity and resilience.

Cultivating a Growth Mindset

A growth mindset, as defined by psychologist Carol Dweck, is the belief that abilities and intelligence can be developed through dedication and hard work. This mindset fosters a love of learning and a resilience that is essential for great accomplishment. Entrepreneurs with a growth mindset view challenges as opportunities to improve and grow.

Overcoming Fear and Self-Doubt

Self-doubt and fear of failure are common barriers to entrepreneurship. To overcome these, it's crucial to reframe your thinking. Instead of viewing failure as a negative outcome, see it as a valuable learning experience. Self-doubt can be mitigated by setting small, achievable goals and celebrating your progress along the way.

Building Resilience

Resilience is the ability to recover from setbacks and persist in the face of challenges. Entrepreneurship is fraught with ups and downs, and resilience is key to navigating these fluctuations. Developing resilience involves maintaining a positive outlook, seeking support from mentors and peers, and staying focused on your long-term vision.

BREAKING FREE: PRACTICAL STEPS TO START YOUR ENTREPRENEURIAL JOURNEY

Identifying Your Passion

The foundation of a successful entrepreneurial venture is a deep passion for what you do. Take time to reflect on your interests, skills, and values. What activities make you lose track of time? What problems do you feel compelled to solve? Your passion will fuel your perseverance and creativity.

Conducting Market Research

Once you've identified your passion, the next step is to explore the market potential. Conduct thorough research to understand your target audience, their needs, and the competitive landscape. This will help you refine your business idea and identify opportunities for differentiation.

Creating a Business Plan

A business plan is a roadmap for your entrepreneurial journey. It outlines your business goals, strategies, and the steps you need to take to achieve them. Key components of a business plan include the following:

1. Executive Summary: A brief overview of your business idea and objectives.

2. Market Analysis: Insights into your target market and competitors.

3. Marketing Strategy: Plans for promoting your business and attracting customers.

4. Operational Plan: Details of how your business will operate on a day-to-day basis.

5. Financial Plan: Projections of your revenue, expenses, and profitability.

Building a Support Network

Entrepreneurship can be a lonely journey, but it doesn't have to be. Surround yourself with a supportive network of mentors, peers, and advisors. Seek out people who have experience in your industry and can provide valuable guidance and feedback.

Securing Funding

Financing is often a significant hurdle for aspiring entrepreneurs. Explore various funding options such as personal savings, loans, grants, and investors. Consider starting small and scaling up gradually as your business gains traction.

Taking the Leap

At some point, you'll need to take the plunge and transition from your nine-to-five job to full-time entrepreneurship. This is a critical and often daunting step. Plan your transition carefully, ensuring you have a financial cushion and a clear action plan for your first few months as an entrepreneur.

STORIES OF SUCCESS: REAL-LIFE EXAMPLES

From Corporate to Creative: The Story of Sarah Blakely

Sarah Blakely, the founder of Spanx, was selling fax machines door-to-door before she revolutionized the hosiery industry.

Despite having no experience in fashion or business, Blakely's determination and innovative spirit led her to create a billion-dollar brand. Her story exemplifies how identifying a common problem and finding a unique solution can lead to entrepreneurial success.

The Garage Startup: The Birth of Apple Inc.

Steve Jobs and Steve Wozniak started Apple in a garage, driven by their passion for technology and innovation. Their journey from humble beginnings to creating one of the world's most valuable companies is a testament to the power of vision, perseverance, and the willingness to take risks.

From Barrister to Barista: The Journey of Howard Schultz

Howard Schultz left his job as a sales executive to join a small coffee shop chain called Starbucks. With a bold vision to bring the Italian coffeehouse experience to America, Schultz transformed Starbucks into a global brand. His story highlights the importance of bold ideas and the courage to pursue them.

OVERCOMING COMMON CHALLENGES

Balancing Risk and Reward

Entrepreneurship involves inherent risks, from financial uncertainty to market competition. Balancing these risks with potential rewards requires careful planning and risk management strategies. Diversify your revenue streams, keep your expenses in check, and continuously adapt to changing market conditions.

Managing Time and Priorities

As an entrepreneur, you'll wear many hats and juggle numerous responsibilities. Effective time management and prioritization are crucial. Use tools like to-do lists, project management software, and delegation to stay organized and focused on high-impact activities.

Handling Failure and Setbacks

Failure is an inevitable part of the entrepreneurial journey. Instead of fearing failure, embrace it as a learning opportunity. Analyze what went wrong, make necessary adjustments, and move forward with renewed determination. Remember, each setback brings you closer to success.

Staying Motivated and Inspired

The entrepreneurial path can be challenging, and maintaining motivation is essential. Set clear, achievable goals, celebrate your milestones, and remind yourself of the reasons you started your journey. Surround yourself with positive influences and seek inspiration from successful entrepreneurs.

EMBRACING THE FUTURE: THE NEW PARADIGM OF WORK

The Rise of the Gig Economy

The gig economy is transforming the traditional employment landscape, offering greater flexibility and opportunities for independent work. Platforms like Uber, Airbnb, and Upwork enable individuals to leverage their skills and assets in new and innovative ways.

The Digital Revolution

Advancements in technology are creating unprecedented opportunities for entrepreneurs. From e-commerce and digital marketing to artificial intelligence and blockchain, the digital revolution is opening new avenues for innovation and business growth.

The Importance of Lifelong Learning

In a rapidly changing world, continuous learning is vital for staying relevant and competitive. Invest in your personal and professional development through courses, workshops, and self-study. Embrace a mindset of curiosity and adaptability.

Breaking free from the nine-to-five and embracing entrepreneurship is a bold and transformative step. It requires courage, resilience, and a willingness to step into the unknown. But the rewards—personal fulfillment, financial independence, and the opportunity to make a meaningful impact—are well worth the effort. Remember, every successful entrepreneur started with a single step. Take that step today. Identify your passion, develop your plan, and begin your journey. The road ahead may be challenging, but it's also filled with limitless possibilities. Your future is in your hands. Dare to dream, take the leap, and create the life you've always envisioned. Your entrepreneurial journey starts now.

PART IV
RESOLUTION

CHAPTER 20

PROCRASTINATION: THE JOURNEY FROM HESITATION TO HEGEMONY

STORY 1: THE INFANT'S EARLY STRUGGLES

In the quiet suburban town of Oakridge, the Johnson family welcomed a new addition, little Emily. From the moment she opened her eyes, Emily was a curious and lively baby, always reaching for the colorful toys her parents dangled above her crib. However, as the months went by, Emily's developmental milestones seemed to lag behind those of her peers. Her parents, Sarah and Mike, began to worry when Emily showed little interest in crawling or walking, preferring instead to lie on her back and gaze at the ceiling.

Sarah read numerous parenting books and consulted pediatricians, but the answer remained elusive. Emily was physically healthy, but her tendency to procrastinate on physical activities was becoming more apparent. When it was time for tummy time, she would cry and resist, rolling over to avoid the effort. The Johnsons tried to encourage her, but Emily's resistance persisted. As Emily grew into a toddler, her procrastination began to affect other areas of her development. She hesitated to speak, relying on gestures and sounds instead. Her day-care teachers noticed that Emily preferred solitary play, avoiding group activities that required interaction and effort. The other children began forming friendships, but Emily remained on the periphery.

Sarah and Mike realized that Emily's early procrastination might have deeper implications for her future. They sought the help of a child psychologist, who explained that Emily's reluctance to engage in challenging activities could stem from an underlying fear of failure. The psychologist recommended a gentle, encouraging approach to help Emily build confidence and overcome her procrastination. The Johnsons implemented a new routine, breaking tasks into smaller, manageable steps and celebrating each of Emily's achievements, no matter how small. They created a positive, supportive environment where Emily felt safe to explore and try new things without fear of judgment. Slowly but surely, Emily began to show progress. She started to crawl, then walk, and eventually, her first words filled the house with joy.

Emily's journey highlighted the importance of early intervention and support in addressing procrastination. By fostering a positive environment and encouraging small victories, the Johnsons helped their daughter overcome her early struggles and set the foundation for a more confident and proactive future.

STORY 2 THE STUDENT'S DILEMMA

Jack was an energetic and bright student in the eighth grade, known for his quick wit and charming personality. However, his teachers and parents noticed a troubling pattern: Jack had a habit of procrastinating on his schoolwork. Assignments that were due in a week were left untouched until the night before, and his grades began to reflect his last-minute efforts. One evening, Jack sat at his desk, staring at the blank page of his book report on *To Kill a Mockingbird*. The assignment was due the next day, and he hadn't read a single page of the book. Instead of starting, Jack found himself scrolling through social media, playing video games, and finding any distraction he could. His mother, Laura, knocked on his door. "Jack, have you started your book report yet?" she asked.

Jack sighed, "I'll get to it, Mom. I just need a break." Laura frowned, knowing that Jack's "breaks" often lasted hours. She decided to have a serious talk with him about his procrastination. They sat down at the kitchen table, and Laura explained how his habit of delaying important tasks was affecting his academic performance and causing unnecessary stress.

"Procrastination is like a snowball, Jack," she said. "The longer you wait, the bigger and more overwhelming it becomes. You need to tackle your assignments bit by bit, rather than all at once." Laura helped Jack create a study schedule, breaking down his assignments into smaller, more manageable tasks. They agreed to set specific times for work and breaks, with the promise of a reward once his tasks were completed. Jack also learned to prioritize his work, starting with the most challenging tasks first.

Over the next few weeks, Jack's grades began to improve. He found that by tackling his assignments in smaller chunks, he could focus better and produce higher-quality work. The stress and anxiety he previously felt began to diminish, and he even had more free time to enjoy his hobbies.

Jack's journey demonstrated how procrastination could significantly impact a student's life, leading to poor academic performance and increased stress. By addressing his procrastination habits early and developing better time management skills, Jack was able to turn his situation around and achieve greater success in school.

STORY 3: THE YOUNG ADULT'S CAREER STRUGGLE

At twenty-five, Ethan was a talented graphic designer with a promising career ahead of him. He had landed a job at a prestigious design firm right out of college and was known for his creative flair and innovative ideas. However, despite his potential, Ethan struggled with procrastination, often leaving projects until the last minute. One day, Ethan's boss, Mr. Thompson, called him into his office. "Ethan, your work is excellent, but I've noticed that you tend to submit your projects right at the deadline. This last-minute rush is affecting the quality of your work and the team's workflow. We need to address this."

Ethan felt a knot in his stomach. He knew his procrastination was becoming a problem, but he felt overwhelmed by the demands of his job. He often found himself distracted by social media, endless emails, and nonurgent tasks, pushing important projects to the back burner.

Mr. Thompson suggested that Ethan attend a time management workshop offered by the company. Reluctantly, Ethan agreed, realizing that he needed to change his habits if he wanted to succeed in his career. The workshop introduced Ethan to the Pomodoro Technique, a time management method that involves working in focused intervals followed by short breaks. He also learned to prioritize tasks using the Eisenhower Matrix, categorizing tasks by urgency and importance. Ethan started implementing these techniques immediately. He broke down his projects into smaller, actionable steps and set specific goals for each work session. He also designated time slots for checking emails and social media, ensuring they didn't interfere with his productive work hours. Gradually, Ethan's productivity improved. He began completing projects ahead of schedule, allowing him time to review and refine his work. His stress levels decreased, and he felt a renewed sense of control over his workload. Mr. Thompson noticed the change and praised Ethan for his improved performance.

Ethan's experience highlighted how procrastination could hinder professional growth and lead to unnecessary stress. By adopting effective time management strategies and changing his approach to work, Ethan was able to overcome his procrastination and excel in his career.

STORY 4: THE MIDDLE-AGED MAN'S MIDLIFE CRISIS

David was a successful lawyer in his midforties, with a thriving practice and a beautiful family. However, as he approached middle age, he began to feel a growing sense of dissatisfaction. The passion he once had for his work was waning, and he found himself procrastinating on important tasks, often pushing them to the last minute. One evening, David sat alone in his office, surrounded by stacks of unfinished case files. He stared at his to-do list, feeling overwhelmed and paralyzed. He knew he needed to make a change, but he didn't know where to start. David's wife, Emily, noticed his struggle and suggested they take a weekend retreat to clear their minds and reflect on their priorities. Reluctantly, David agreed, hoping a change of scenery might help.

During the retreat, David had a chance to disconnect from his daily grind and reflect on his life. He realized that his procrastination was a symptom of a deeper issue: he had lost sight of his goals and passions. He was simply going through the motions, without any real sense of purpose. Emily encouraged David to consider what truly made him happy and fulfilled. They talked about his long-forgotten dreams and passions, and David began to see a path forward. He decided to make a conscious effort to reconnect with his values and priorities. David returned to work with a renewed sense of purpose. He began delegating tasks more effectively, focusing on the cases that truly mattered to him. He also set aside time for self-care, hobbies, and family, ensuring he had a balanced life. Over time, David's procrastination diminished, and he felt more engaged and motivated in his work. He found that by aligning his tasks with his values and passions, he could overcome his midlife crisis and regain his sense of purpose.

David's story illustrated how procrastination could be a sign of deeper dissatisfaction and a lack of purpose. By taking the time to reflect and realign his priorities, David was able to overcome his procrastination and find fulfillment in his work and personal life.

STORY 5: THE ELDERLY WOMAN'S REFLECTIONS

At seventy-five, Margaret had lived a full life, filled with ups and downs, successes, and failures. As she sat in her cozy living room, surrounded by photos of her children and grandchildren, she couldn't help but reflect on the choices she had made over the years. One recurring theme stood out: procrastination. Margaret had always been a procrastinator, putting off tasks and decisions until the last possible moment. In her younger years, it had affected her education and career, leading to missed opportunities and unfulfilled potential. As she grew older, procrastination had seeped into other areas of her life, from managing her finances to maintaining her health.

Now, in her twilight years, Margaret could see the long-term impact of her procrastination. She had always intended to travel the world, but she had put it off, thinking there would always be time. Her health had started to decline, making those dreams increasingly unattainable. One day, her granddaughter, Lily, visited and asked Margaret about her life experiences. As they talked, Margaret shared her regrets and lessons learned. She told Lily about the importance of taking action and not letting fear or uncertainty lead to procrastination. "Life is too short to put things off," Margaret said. "I've learned that it's better to take a chance and fail than to live with the regret of never trying."

Inspired by her grandmother's wisdom, Lily decided to make the most of her own life. She pursued her passions with vigor, taking risks and embracing new opportunities. Margaret watched with pride as Lily achieved her dreams, knowing that her own experiences had taught her granddaughter a valuable lesson.

Margaret's story underscored how procrastination could have long-lasting effects on one's life, leading to missed opportunities and unfulfilled dreams. Her reflections served as a reminder to live life fully and seize the moment, ensuring that regrets are few and far between.

Procrastination affects individuals at various stages of life, from infancy to old age. Each story highlights the different ways procrastination can impact our lives, emphasizing the importance of addressing this habit early and developing strategies to overcome it. By understanding the consequences of procrastination and taking proactive steps to manage our time and priorities, we can lead more fulfilling and successful lives.

PROCRASTINATION: THE BARRIER BETWEEN PAIN AND PLEASURE, HESITATION AND HEGEMONY

Procrastination is a universal experience that affects everyone at some point in their lives. It is the act of delaying or postponing tasks, often to the point of experiencing stress, anxiety, and guilt. This habit creates a significant barrier between pain and pleasure, preventing us from moving from a state of discomfort to one of fulfillment and satisfaction. Understanding the journey from pain to pleasure and the role procrastination plays can help us develop strategies to overcome this common obstacle.

The Pain of Procrastination

Procrastination often starts with an avoidance of tasks that are perceived as difficult, unpleasant, or overwhelming. This avoidance creates immediate relief, which is why procrastination is so appealing. However, the temporary pleasure of avoidance quickly turns into pain as deadlines approach, responsibilities pile up, and the pressure to perform intensifies.

❶ STRESS AND ANXIETY

Procrastination leads to increased stress and anxiety as we realize that we are running out of time to complete our tasks. The closer we get to the deadline, the more anxious we become, which can affect our mental and physical health.

❷ DECREASED PRODUCTIVITY

When we procrastinate, we waste valuable time that could be spent on productive activities. This leads to a decrease in overall productivity, as tasks that could have been completed in a timely manner now require rushed efforts and compromised quality.

❸ GUILT AND SELF-DOUBT

The habit of procrastination often leads to feelings of guilt and self-doubt. We know that we should be working on our tasks, but the fact that we aren't can make us feel inadequate and question our abilities.

The Pleasure of Accomplishment

On the other side of procrastination lies the pleasure of accomplishment. Completing tasks on time and to the best of our ability brings a sense of satisfaction, achievement, and pride. This positive reinforcement can boost our confidence and motivate us to take on new challenges.

🏵 SENSE OF ACHIEVEMENT

Successfully completing tasks provides a sense of achievement and fulfillment. This positive outcome reinforces our ability to tackle future tasks with confidence.

🏵 REDUCED STRESS

Finishing tasks on time reduces stress and anxiety, leading to improved mental and physical health. We can enjoy our free time without the looming pressure of unfinished work.

🏵 INCREASED PRODUCTIVITY

When we overcome procrastination, we become more productive. Completing tasks efficiently allows us to take on more projects, learn new skills, and achieve our goals.

Overcoming Procrastination: Strategies and Tips

Breaking the cycle of procrastination requires understanding why we procrastinate and implementing strategies to overcome this habit. Here are several ways to help ourselves remain motivated and avoid procrastination:

🏵 SET CLEAR GOALS

Setting clear, achievable goals can provide direction and purpose. Break down large tasks into smaller, manageable steps, and set deadlines for each step. This makes the task less overwhelming and more achievable.

❷ PRIORITIZE TASKS

Prioritizing tasks based on urgency and importance can help us focus on what needs to be done first. Use tools like the Eisenhower Matrix to categorize tasks and decide where to start.

❸ CREATE A SCHEDULE

Creating a schedule can help manage time effectively. Allocate specific times for work, breaks, and leisure activities. Stick to the schedule as closely as possible to build a routine and stay on track.

❹ ELIMINATE DISTRACTIONS

Identify and eliminate distractions that hinder productivity. This may include turning off notifications, creating a dedicated workspace, and setting boundaries with family and friends during work hours.

❺ USE THE POMODORO TECHNIQUE

The Pomodoro Technique involves working in focused intervals (usually twenty-five minutes) followed by a short break. This method helps maintain concentration and prevents burnout.

❻ REWARD YOURSELF

Rewarding yourself for completing tasks can provide motivation. Set up a system of rewards for reaching milestones, whether it's a treat, a break, or an activity you enjoy.

❼ PRACTICE SELF-COMPASSION

Be kind to yourself when you encounter setbacks. Understand

that procrastination is a common experience and use it as an opportunity to learn and grow. Self-compassion can help reduce the guilt and self-doubt associated with procrastination.

🏵 SEEK ACCOUNTABILITY

Having someone to hold you accountable can be a powerful motivator. Share your goals and progress with a friend, family member, or mentor who can provide encouragement and support.

FROM PAIN TO PLEASURE: THE JOURNEY FROM HESITATION TO HEGEMONY

The journey from pain to pleasure involves recognizing the discomfort caused by procrastination and taking proactive steps to overcome it. By implementing the strategies outlined above, we can break free from the cycle of procrastination and move toward a more fulfilling and productive life.

Recognize the Pain

The first step is to recognize the pain caused by procrastination. Acknowledge the stress, anxiety, and guilt that come with delaying tasks. This awareness can serve as a motivator to change.

Visualize the Pleasure

Visualize the pleasure and satisfaction that come with completing tasks on time. Imagine the sense of achievement, reduced stress, and increased productivity. This positive visualization can inspire action.

Take Small Steps

Start with small, manageable steps. Break down tasks into smaller parts and tackle them one at a time. Each small victory builds momentum and confidence.

Build a Routine

Building a routine can help create consistency and reduce the likelihood of procrastination. Establish regular work hours and stick to them, even when motivation is low.

Reflect and Adjust

Regularly reflect on your progress and adjust your strategies as needed. Identify what works and what doesn't, and make changes to improve your productivity.

Procrastination is a significant barrier that stands between the pain of inaction and the pleasure of accomplishment. It can lead to stress, anxiety, decreased productivity, and feelings of guilt and self-doubt. However, by understanding the reasons behind procrastination and implementing effective strategies, we can overcome this habit and move toward a more fulfilling and productive life. Setting clear goals, prioritizing tasks, creating a schedule, eliminating distractions, using the Pomodoro Technique, rewarding ourselves, practicing self-compassion, and seeking accountability are all powerful tools to combat procrastination.

The journey from pain to pleasure involves recognizing the discomfort caused by procrastination, visualizing the benefits of accomplishment, taking small steps, building a routine, and regularly reflecting and adjusting our approach. By taking proactive steps to address procrastination, we can unlock our full potential, achieve our goals, and enjoy the satisfaction and pleasure that come with a life of accomplishment and productivity.

CHAPTER 21

DEAR POSTERITY: SECURING A FUTURE FOR POSTERITY—ADDRESSING CLIMATE CHANGE, EMBRACING VEGANISM, AND APOLOGIZING TO FUTURE GENERATIONS

Posterity, the generations that will come after us, is a concept that demands our attention and responsibility. Our actions today have far-reaching consequences, and it is our duty to ensure that the world we leave behind is one where future generations can thrive. Climate change, a pressing issue of our time, is a significant threat to this vision. Moreover, adopting sustainable lifestyles, such as veganism, can play a crucial role in mitigating these challenges. This chapter explores why climate change is the most critical issue to address today, discusses the importance of veganism for our posterity, and offers an apology to future generations for the environmental degradation we have caused. Additionally, it includes quotes from influential figures about posterity and suggests ways we can help future generations recover from our environmental missteps.

WHY CLIMATE CHANGE IS THE MOST IMPORTANT ISSUE

The Urgency of Climate Change

Climate change refers to long-term changes in temperature, precipitation, and weather patterns, primarily due to human activities such as burning fossil fuels, deforestation, and industrial processes. The scientific consensus is clear: climate change is real, it is happening now, and it poses an existential threat to humanity and the planet.

Impacts of Climate Change

1. Rising Temperatures: Global temperatures are rising at an unprecedented rate. This leads to more frequent and severe heat waves, affecting human health, agriculture, and ecosystems.

2. Melting Ice Caps and Rising Sea Levels: The polar ice caps and glaciers are melting, contributing to rising sea levels. This threatens coastal communities with flooding and displacement.

3. Extreme Weather Events: Climate change increases the frequency and intensity of extreme weather events such as hurricanes, droughts, and wildfires, causing widespread destruction and loss of life.

4. Biodiversity Loss: Many species are unable to adapt quickly enough to changing climates, leading to extinc-

tion. This loss of biodiversity affects ecosystems and human livelihoods.

5. Ocean Acidification: Increased carbon dioxide (CO2) absorption by the oceans is causing acidification, which harms marine life, particularly coral reefs and shellfish.

The Consequences of Inaction

If we fail to address climate change, the consequences will be catastrophic:

1. Human Suffering: Failure to address climate change will lead to increased heat-related illnesses, food and water shortages, and displacement due to rising sea levels and extreme weather events.

2. Economic Costs: Damage to infrastructure, decreased agricultural productivity, and the costs of disaster response and recovery will strain economies.

3. Environmental Collapse: Inaction regarding climate change will result in irreversible damage to ecosystems and the extinction of countless species, leading to a less resilient planet.

4. Social and Political Unrest: Resource scarcity and displacement can lead to conflicts, exacerbating social and political instability.

THE ROLE OF VEGANISM IN ADDRESSING CLIMATE CHANGE

Environmental Benefits of Veganism

Veganism, a lifestyle that excludes all animal products, can significantly reduce our environmental footprint. The livestock industry is a major contributor to greenhouse gas emissions, deforestation, and water pollution. By adopting a vegan diet, here's what we can do:

1. Reduce Greenhouse Gas Emissions: Livestock farming produces methane and nitrous oxide, potent greenhouse gases. A plant-based diet significantly lowers these emissions.

2. Save Water: Animal agriculture is water intensive. Producing plant-based foods requires far less water than producing meat and dairy.

3. Conserve Land: Livestock farming requires vast amounts of land for grazing and growing feed crops. Shifting to plant-based diets can free up land for reforestation and wildlife habitats.

4. Protect Biodiversity: Deforestation for animal agriculture destroys habitats and threatens species. A vegan diet can help preserve biodiversity.

Health Benefits of Veganism

In addition to environmental benefits, veganism offers significant health advantages:

1. Reduced Risk of Chronic Diseases: Plant-based diets are linked to lower risks of heart disease, hypertension, type 2 diabetes, and certain cancers.

2. Weight Management: Vegan diets are often lower in calories and saturated fats, helping with weight management and reducing obesity rates.

3. Improved Digestive Health: High fiber content in plant-based diets promotes healthy digestion and reduces the risk of gastrointestinal diseases.

APOLOGY TO FUTURE GENERATIONS

Dear Future Generations,

We owe you an apology. As we reflect on the state of our planet, we recognize the immense burden we have placed on you. Our actions, driven by short-term gains and convenience, have resulted in a world facing unprecedented environmental challenges. We failed to heed the warnings of scientists, activists, and indigenous communities who urged us to protect our Earth.

We are sorry for the rising temperatures that make summers unbearable and winters unpredictable. We apologize for the melting ice caps that threaten coastal cities and the homes of countless species. We regret the pollution of our air and water, and the loss of biodiversity that makes our world less vibrant and resilient. We did not do enough to mitigate the impacts of climate change. We prioritized economic growth over ecological sustainability, and in doing so, we jeopardized your future. Our reliance on fossil fuels, deforestation, and unsustainable agricultural practices have left you with a planet in crisis. We are also sorry for the slow progress in addressing these issues. While some of us have fought for change, it has not been enough. Policies were not enacted quickly enough, and collective action was often hindered by political and economic interests.

As we strive to do better, we find inspiration in the words of those who have spoken about the importance of caring for future generations:

> *We do not inherit the Earth from our ancestors; we borrow it from our children.*
>
> **—NATIVE AMERICAN PROVERB**
>
> *The true meaning of life is to plant trees, under whose shade you do not expect to sit.*
>
> **—NELSON HENDERSON**
>
> *We have a single mission: to protect and hand on the planet to the next generation.*
>
> **—FRANÇOIS HOLLANDE**
>
> *The greatest threat to our planet is the belief that someone else will save it.*
>
> **—ROBERT SWAN**
>
> *He who plants a tree, plants a hope.*
>
> **—LUCY LARCOM**

THE FUTURE WE ENVISION

The future we envision is one where humanity lives in harmony with nature. It is a world where renewable energy powers our homes and industries, where sustainable agriculture feeds the population, and where natural habitats are preserved for future generations. In this future, people understand the interconnectedness of all life and act with a sense of responsibility toward the planet. This future also values diversity and inclusivity, recognizing that the solutions to our environmental challenges require the participation of all communities. It is a world where education and innovation drive progress, and where leaders prioritize the long-term health of the planet over short-term gains.

In this envisioned future, cities are green and sustainable, with efficient public transportation systems, green spaces, and clean air. Rural areas thrive with regenerative agriculture practices that restore soil health and biodiversity. Oceans are protected from pollution and overfishing, ensuring the survival of marine life.

Securing a future for posterity requires immediate and sustained action. Climate change is the most pressing issue we face, and addressing it demands a collective effort from all of us. Adopting sustainable lifestyles, such as veganism, can significantly reduce our environmental impact and contribute to a healthier planet. We must also acknowledge our mistakes and apologize to future generations for the damage we have caused. By drawing inspiration from influential figures and implementing solutions that prioritize sustainability, we can create a better future for those who come after us. The path forward is challenging, but it is also filled with opportunities for innovation, growth, and collaboration. Together, we can build a world where future generations can thrive, free from the environmental burdens we face today. Let us commit to this vision and take the necessary steps to make it a reality.

Here are fifty data-driven questions to help you understand the impact of climate change:

1. Did you know that the global average temperature has increased by 1.2°C since the late nineteenth century?

2. Did you know that the five warmest years on record have all occurred since 2015?

3. Did you know that 2020 tied with 2016 as the warmest year on record?

4. Did you know that the Greenland and Antarctic ice sheets are losing mass at an accelerating rate, with Greenland losing an average of 279 gigatons of ice per year between 1993 and 2019?

5. Did you know that global sea levels have risen about eight inches (twenty centimeters) since 1880, with the rate of rise increasing in recent decades?

6. Did you know that sea level rise is causing coastal erosion, increased flooding, and the loss of habitat for plants, animals, and even people?

7. Did you know that ocean acidification caused by the absorption of CO_2 has increased by 30 percent since the beginning of the Industrial Revolution?

8. Did you know that coral reefs are bleaching and dying at unprecedented rates due to rising ocean temperatures and acidification?

9. Did you know that nearly 50 percent of the world's coral reefs have been lost in the past thirty years?

10. Did you know that the Arctic sea ice extent has decreased by about 40 percent since 1979?

11. Did you know that the thawing of Arctic permafrost releases methane, a potent greenhouse gas, exacerbating climate change?

12. Did you know that wildfires in the western United States have increased fivefold since the 1970s due to warmer temperatures and drier conditions?

13. Did you know that 2020 saw a record number of named storms in the Atlantic hurricane season, with thirty named storms and twelve making landfall in the US?

14. Did you know that climate change is expected to displace more than 143 million people by 2050 due to extreme weather, sea level rise, and agricultural disruption?

15. Did you know that the World Health Organization estimates climate change will cause approximately 250,000 additional deaths per year between 2030 and 2050 due to malnutrition, malaria, diarrhea, and heat stress?

16. Did you know that climate change is expected to push 100 million people into extreme poverty by 2030?

17. Did you know that the agriculture sector contributes around 10 percent of global greenhouse gas emissions?

18. Did you know that livestock farming is responsible for 14.5 percent of global greenhouse gas emissions—more than all cars, planes, trains, and ships combined?

19. Did you know that the production of a kilogram of beef emits the equivalent of 27 kilograms of CO_2—compared to just 2.5 kilograms for a kilogram of wheat?

20. Did you know that deforestation contributes to about 10 to 15 percent of global greenhouse gas emissions, and the Amazon rainforest is losing the equivalent of a football field of forest every minute?

21. Did you know that switching to a plant-based diet can reduce an individual's carbon footprint from food by up to 73 percent?

22. Did you know that renewable energy sources like wind and solar are now cheaper than coal and natural gas in most regions?

23. Did you know that in 2019, renewables provided more than 72 percent of new global electricity generation capacity?

24. Did you know that energy efficiency improvements could deliver more than 40 percent of the greenhouse gas emissions reductions needed to meet global climate goals?

25. Did you know that the transportation sector is responsible for about 24 percent of global CO_2 emissions from fuel combustion?

26. Did you know that electric vehicles produce fewer greenhouse gases and air pollutants over their lifetime than petrol or diesel cars, even when taking into account the electricity used for charging?

27. Did you know that buildings and their construction account for 36 percent of global energy use and 39 percent of energy-related CO_2 emissions annually?

28. Did you know that planting trees and reforestation could remove around ten to fifteen gigatons of CO_2 per year, roughly equivalent to 25 percent of current annual fossil fuel emissions?

29. Did you know that urban areas are responsible for about 70 percent of global CO_2 emissions?

30. Did you know that the average global temperature increase of 2°C could result in the loss of 99 percent of coral reefs?

31. Did you know that air pollution from burning fossil fuels kills an estimated 8.7 million people worldwide each year?

32. Did you know that by 2030, the global demand for water is projected to exceed sustainable supply by 40 percent?

33. Did you know that approximately 1.6 billion people currently live in areas of water scarcity, a number expected to double by 2025?

34. Did you know that the production and use of single-use plastics contribute significantly to climate change, with plastics estimated to account for 4 to 8 percent of global oil consumption?

35. Did you know that reducing food waste could cut global greenhouse gas emissions by 8 percent?

36. Did you know that climate change could reduce global crop yields by up to 30 percent by 2050, leading to increased food insecurity?

37. Did you know that the global fashion industry is responsible for about 10 percent of annual global carbon emissions?

38. Did you know that fast fashion produces 92 million tons of waste per year and consumes 79 trillion liters of water?

39. Did you know that global warming is causing the spread of diseases like malaria and dengue fever to new regions, as warmer temperatures allow mosquitoes to survive in previously inhospitable areas?

40. Did you know that by 2050, the global energy demand is expected to increase by nearly 50 percent, requiring a massive shift to renewable energy to meet climate goals?

41. Did you know that the construction of a new wind turbine pays for itself within six months in terms of the energy it generates versus the energy used to build it?

42. Did you know that 1.5°C of global warming could expose 14 percent of the world's population to severe heat waves at least once every five years?

43. Did you know that climate change could force more than a million species to face extinction by 2050 if current trends continue?

44. Did you know that protecting and restoring wetlands can significantly reduce the impacts of flooding and storms, helping to mitigate climate change?

45. Did you know that investing in green infrastructure, such as parks and green roofs, can improve urban resilience to climate change while providing social and economic benefits?

46. Did you know that the Paris Agreement aims to limit global warming to well below 2°C, with efforts to limit the increase to 1.5°C, but current policies are projected to result in about 2.9°C of warming by 2100?

47. Did you know that 2020 was one of the three warmest years on record despite the cooling effects of La Niña, highlighting the long-term trend of global warming?

48. Did you know that reducing meat consumption and food waste can decrease global greenhouse gas emissions by up to 70 percent by 2050?

49. Did you know that the world's oceans absorb about 90 percent of the excess heat generated by greenhouse gas emissions, causing more frequent and intense marine heatwaves?

50. Did you know that achieving net-zero carbon emissions by 2050 is critical to prevent the worst impacts of climate change and ensure a sustainable future for posterity?

Here are fifty actionable steps that future generations can take to prevent Earth and humanity from facing extinction due to climate change:

1. Transition to Renewable Energy: Invest in and adopt solar, wind, and other renewable energy sources.

2. Create Energy Efficiency: Implement energy-efficient technologies and practices in homes, buildings, and industries.

3. Electrify Transportation: Promote electric vehicles and invest in public transportation infrastructure.

4. Promote Sustainable Agriculture: Support regenerative farming practices and reduce the use of chemical fertilizers and pesticides.

5. Reduce Meat Consumption: Shift toward plant-based diets to lower greenhouse gas emissions from livestock.

6. Practice Zero Waste: Adopt zero-waste practices; reduce, reuse, and recycle materials to minimize landfill waste.

7. Conserve Water: Implement water-saving technologies and practices to conserve water resources.

8. Support Reforestation: Plant trees and restore forests to absorb CO_2 and enhance biodiversity.

9. Protect Wetlands: Preserve and restore wetlands to act as carbon sinks and prevent flooding.

10. Protect the Oceans: Implement policies to protect marine ecosystems and reduce overfishing and pollution.

11. Establish Sustainable Fisheries: Support sustainable fishing practices to ensure the long-term health of marine life.

12. Implement Green Building Design: Construct energy-efficient and sustainable buildings using eco-friendly materials.

13. Encourage Urban Greening: Increase green spaces in urban areas to reduce heat islands and improve air quality.

14. Research Renewable Energy: Invest in research and development of advanced renewable energy technologies.

15. Educate on Climate: Educate communities about climate change and promote sustainable living practices.

16. Advocate for Climate Policy: Push for strong climate policies and international agreements to reduce emissions.

17. Support Clean Energy Initiatives: Encourage governments and businesses to invest in clean energy projects.

18. Implement Carbon Pricing: Implement carbon pricing mechanisms to incentivize the reduction of greenhouse gas emissions.

19. Support Climate Resilience: Build resilient infrastructure and communities to withstand the impacts of climate change.

20. Promote Circular Economy: Transition to a circular economy where waste is minimized and resources are reused.

21. Reduce Air Travel: Limit air travel and promote alternative modes of transportation to reduce carbon footprints.

22. Invest in Public Transit: Develop and expand public transportation systems to reduce reliance on private vehicles.

23. Promote Biking and Walking: Create bike lanes and pedestrian-friendly infrastructure to encourage nonmotorized transport.

24. Develop Smart Grids: Implement smart grid technologies to optimize energy use and integrate renewable energy sources.

25. Implement Sustainable Tourism: Promote eco-friendly tourism practices that protect natural resources.

26. Encourage Telecommuting: Support remote work and telecommuting to reduce transportation emissions.

27. Encourage Sustainable Fashion: Support sustainable fashion brands and practices that reduce the environmental impact of clothing production.

28. Support Local Products: Buy locally produced goods to reduce transportation emissions and support local economies.

29. Invest in Carbon Capture: Support the development and deployment of carbon capture and storage technologies.

30. Reduce Plastic Use: Minimize the use of single-use plastics and promote biodegradable alternatives.

31. Protect Biodiversity: Implement conservation strategies to protect endangered species and ecosystems.

32. Promote Climate Justice: Ensure that climate policies address social inequalities and support vulnerable communities.

33. Support Indigenous Rights: Recognize and support the land rights of Indigenous peoples who protect critical ecosystems.

34. Adopt Sustainable Fishing: Implement sustainable fishing practices to prevent overfishing and protect marine biodiversity.

35. Reduce Food Waste: Implement measures to reduce food waste at the production, retail, and consumer levels.

36. Encourage Community Gardens: Promote community gardening projects to increase local food production and reduce emissions.

37. Promote Agroforestry: Integrate trees into agricultural landscapes to sequester carbon and improve soil health.

38. Support Climate-Smart Agriculture: Adopt agricultural practices that increase resilience to climate impacts.

39. Reduce Industrial Emissions: Implement cleaner production technologies and practices to reduce industrial greenhouse gas emissions.

40. Invest in Green Technologies: Support the development and deployment of technologies that reduce environmental impact.

41. Promote Renewable Energy Jobs: Encourage job creation in the renewable energy sector to support a green economy.

42. Implement Sustainable Land Use: Develop land-use policies that prioritize conservation and sustainable development.

43. Encourage Reforestation: Support large-scale reforestation projects to sequester carbon and restore ecosystems.

44. Support Marine Conservation: Advocate for marine protected areas and policies that reduce ocean pollution.

45. Invest in Clean Water: Develop technologies and infrastructure to ensure access to clean and safe drinking water.

46. Promote Energy Storage: Invest in energy storage solutions to enhance the reliability and efficiency of renewable energy.

47. Encourage Citizen Science: Engage communities in monitoring and reporting environmental changes to support climate research.

48. Develop Climate-Resilient Crops: Invest in the development of crops that can withstand climate extremes.

49. Promote Sustainable Finance: Encourage investment in sustainable and green financial products and practices.

50. Support Climate Action Plans: Develop and implement comprehensive climate action plans at local, national, and global levels to achieve carbon neutrality.

By taking these steps, future generations can help mitigate the impacts of climate change and build a sustainable, resilient, and thriving planet for themselves and those who come after them.

ARE LITHIUM BATTERIES A FARCE, OR A BOON FOR THE ENVIRONMENT?

Lithium-ion batteries have become ubiquitous in our modern world, powering everything from smartphones and laptops to electric vehicles (EVs) and renewable energy storage systems. However, the question arises: are lithium batteries truly beneficial for the environment, or are they merely a stopgap measure that brings its own set of problems? This section explores the environmental impact of lithium batteries, how lithium mining can be done sustainably, and the best practices for disposing of and recycling these batteries.

The Environmental Impact of Lithium Batteries

Lithium-ion batteries have several advantages over traditional energy storage solutions. They have a higher energy density, longer lifespan, and lower self-discharge rate compared to older technologies like nickel-cadmium or lead-acid batteries. These attributes make them particularly suitable for applications where efficiency and longevity are critical, such as in electric vehicles and renewable energy storage systems. From an environmental perspective, lithium-ion batteries play a significant role in reducing greenhouse gas emissions.

Electric vehicles, powered by lithium batteries, emit zero tailpipe emissions, and when charged with electricity from renewable sources, their overall carbon footprint is dramatically lower than that of internal combustion engine vehicles. Similarly, lithium batteries enable the storage of solar and wind energy, making these intermittent renewable sources more reliable and reducing the reliance on fossil fuels. However, the production and disposal of lithium-ion batteries are not without environmental concerns. The extraction of lithium and other critical materials such as cobalt, nickel, and manganese involves mining practices that can be environmentally damaging. These processes can lead to soil degradation, water pollution, and loss of biodiversity. Moreover, improper disposal of lithium batteries can result in toxic chemicals leaching into the soil and water, posing significant environmental and health risks.

Sustainable Lithium Mining

To mitigate the environmental impact of lithium mining, we can adopt several sustainable practices:

1. **Direct Lithium Extraction (DLE):** This method involves extracting lithium directly from brine, using a series of chemical processes that are more efficient and less water intensive than traditional evaporation ponds. DLE reduces the environmental footprint and allows for lithium extraction from a broader range of sources, including geothermal brine and oil field brine.

2. **Recycling and Reuse:** Recycling lithium from used batteries can significantly reduce the need for new lithium mining. Efficient recycling processes can recover up to 95 percent of the lithium and other valuable materials, reducing the demand for virgin resources and minimizing environmental impact.

3. **Closed-Loop Water Systems:** Implementing closed-loop water systems in mining operations can prevent water contamination and reduce water usage. These systems recycle water used in the extraction process, minimizing the impact on local water resources.

4. **Responsible Mining Standards:** Adopting and adhering to responsible mining standards, such as those outlined by the Initiative for Responsible Mining Assurance (IRMA), can ensure that mining practices are environmentally sound and socially responsible. These standards cover a wide range of criteria, including waste management, water usage, and community engagement.

Proper Disposal and Recycling of Lithium Batteries

The life cycle of a lithium-ion battery does not end when it wears out. Proper disposal and recycling are crucial to minimize environmental impact and recover valuable materials. Here are some best practices:

1. **Battery Collection Programs:** Establishing comprehensive battery collection programs can ensure that used batteries are collected and sent to recycling facilities rather than ending up in landfills. Public awareness campaigns and convenient drop-off locations can encourage consumers to participate in these programs.

2. **Advanced Recycling Technologies:** Investing in advanced recycling technologies can improve the efficiency and effectiveness of lithium battery recycling. Techniques such as hydrometallurgical and pyrometallurgical processes can recover lithium, cobalt, nickel, and other valuable materials from used batteries.

3. **Second-Life Applications:** Before recycling, used lithium batteries can be repurposed for second-life applications. For example, batteries that no longer meet the high performance standards for EVs can be used in less demanding applications, such as stationary energy storage for renewable energy systems.

4. **Regulatory Frameworks:** Governments can implement regulatory frameworks that mandate the recycling of lithium batteries and provide incentives for companies to develop and adopt sustainable recycling practices. Regulations can also ensure that manufacturers take responsi-

bility for the entire life cycle of their products, promoting the design of batteries that are easier to recycle.

Lithium-ion batteries are not a farce; they are a crucial component in the transition to a more sustainable and low-carbon future. While they do have environmental impacts, particularly related to mining and disposal, these can be mitigated through sustainable practices and proper recycling. Direct Lithium Extraction (DLE), responsible mining standards, and closed-loop water systems are some of the ways to make lithium mining more environmentally friendly. Proper disposal and recycling of lithium batteries are equally important. Battery collection programs, advanced recycling technologies, second-life applications, and regulatory frameworks can all contribute to reducing the environmental footprint of lithium batteries.

While lithium-ion batteries are not without their challenges, they offer significant environmental benefits, particularly in reducing greenhouse gas emissions and enabling the widespread adoption of renewable energy. By adopting sustainable mining practices and ensuring proper disposal and recycling, we can harness the advantages of lithium batteries while minimizing their environmental impact, thus making them a viable solution for a greener future.

CHAPTER 22

AIKIDO

Aikido, a modern Japanese martial art developed by Morihei Ueshiba, emphasizes harmony, blending, and the redirection of an opponent's energy to neutralize threats without causing harm. These principles can be highly effective in the world of entrepreneurship, where founders often face challenges and competition. By leveraging the strengths of their adversaries, entrepreneurs can turn potential obstacles into opportunities for growth and innovation.

UNDERSTANDING AIKIDO

Aikido, which translates to "the way of harmony with the spirit," focuses on using an opponent's force against them. Instead of meeting force with force, aikido practitioners blend with the attacker's movements and redirect their energy. This approach minimizes conflict and maximizes efficiency, promoting a peaceful resolution. In entrepreneurship, the adversaries might not be physical opponents but could be competitors, market challenges, or internal conflicts. By applying aikido principles, entrepreneurs can navigate these challenges more effectively, creating synergies and turning potential threats into advantages.

Key Aikido Principles and Their Application in Entrepreneurship

❶ BLENDING AND REDIRECTION

In aikido, blending involves moving with the attacker's energy rather than opposing it. For entrepreneurs, this can mean aligning with market trends and customer needs instead of resisting them. Redirection, on the other hand, is about guiding the adversary's force in a way that neutralizes the threat and benefits the defender.

EXAMPLE: A small startup might face stiff competition from a larger, well-established company. Instead of directly competing, the startup could identify a niche market that the larger company is overlooking. By blending with market needs and redirecting their efforts, the startup can capture a loyal customer base that values personalized service and innovation.

❷ USING MINIMAL FORCE

Aikido teaches the use of minimal force to achieve maximum effect. In business, this translates to leveraging available resources efficiently and focusing on core strengths rather than spreading efforts too thin.

EXAMPLE: A tech startup with limited funding could focus on developing a single high-quality product rather than multiple mediocre ones. By concentrating their efforts and resources on what they do best, they can create a strong market presence and attract investment.

❸ MAINTAINING BALANCE

Balance is crucial in aikido, as it allows practitioners to remain stable and responsive. Entrepreneurs must also maintain a balance between innovation and practicality, risk and caution, and work and life.

EXAMPLE An entrepreneur might face the temptation to take on too many projects at once. By maintaining balance and prioritizing the most promising opportunities, they can ensure steady progress and avoid burnout.

❹ TURNING OPPONENTS INTO ALLIES

One of the most powerful aikido principles is transforming an opponent's energy into a cooperative force. In business, this can mean turning competitors into collaborators or finding common ground with critics.

EXAMPLE Two competing startups in the same industry might find it beneficial to collaborate on a joint venture that leverages their combined strengths. This partnership can lead to innovative solutions and a stronger market position for both parties.

Practical Applications of Aikido in Entrepreneurship

❶ MARKET RESEARCH AND ADAPTATION

By understanding and adapting to market trends, entrepreneurs can blend with the existing business environment. This involves staying informed about customer preferences, technological advancements, and industry shifts. Adapting to these changes can provide a competitive edge.

EXAMPLE When the COVID-19 pandemic hit, many businesses had to pivot to survive. Restaurants started offering delivery services, and fitness trainers moved their classes online. Those who quickly adapted to the new normal were able to thrive despite the challenging circumstances.

❷ CONFLICT RESOLUTION AND NEGOTIATION

In business, conflicts are inevitable—whether with partners, employees, or clients. Aikido teaches the importance of resolving conflicts without escalating them. Entrepreneurs can use active listening, empathy, and compromise to find mutually beneficial solutions.

EXAMPLE A founder might have a disagreement with a cofounder about the direction of the company. Instead of engaging in a power struggle, the founder could use aikido principles to understand the cofounder's perspective, find common ground, and develop a strategy that incorporates both viewpoints.

❸ RESOURCE MANAGEMENT

Efficient use of resources is critical for any startup. By focusing on core strengths and using minimal force, entrepreneurs can achieve maximum impact with limited resources. This might involve outsourcing non-core activities, automating processes, or leveraging technology.

EXAMPLE A startup with a small team could use project management tools to streamline their workflow and ensure that everyone is working efficiently. By doing so, they can achieve more with less and stay competitive.

❹ STRATEGIC PARTNERSHIPS

Building alliances and partnerships can help entrepreneurs

leverage the strengths of others. By turning potential competitors into allies, businesses can access new markets, share resources, and innovate more effectively.

EXAMPLE A startup developing eco-friendly packaging might partner with a large retailer committed to sustainability. This partnership can provide the startup with a steady customer base and the retailer with innovative solutions that enhance their brand image.

A STORY OF AIKIDO IN ENTREPRENEURSHIP

Turning Competition into Collaboration: The Story of GreenTech Innovations

In a bustling city, Alex Martinez, an aspiring entrepreneur, dreamt of creating a sustainable energy solution that could power homes efficiently and affordably. He founded GreenTech Innovations, a startup focused on developing cutting-edge solar panels. However, the market was saturated with established companies, making it challenging for a new player to gain traction. Alex soon realized that direct competition with these giants was futile. His small team and limited resources couldn't match the scale and reach of the industry leaders. But Alex was an avid practitioner of aikido and believed in its principles of harmony and redirection.

Instead of viewing the established companies as adversaries, Alex saw an opportunity to learn from them. He began attending industry conferences and networking events, not to compete but to understand their strengths and weaknesses. He discovered that while the big companies had vast resources, they were often slow to innovate and adapt to new technologies. One day, Alex met Sarah, a senior executive from SolarMax, one of the largest players in the market. During their conversation, Alex learned that SolarMax was facing challenges in integrating new, efficient technologies into their existing product line. They had the resources but lacked the agility to innovate quickly.

Alex saw an opportunity to apply his aikido principles. He proposed a collaboration where GreenTech Innovations would act as a research and development partner for SolarMax. His agile team could rapidly develop and test new technologies, which SolarMax could then scale and distribute through their established channels. Sarah was intrigued by the idea. She recognized the potential benefits of combining SolarMax's resources with GreenTech's innovative capabilities.

They agreed to a partnership, with SolarMax providing funding and market access, while GreenTech focused on research and development. This collaboration allowed GreenTech to thrive. With SolarMax's support, they could innovate faster and bring cutting-edge solar technology to the market. SolarMax, in turn, benefited from the fresh ideas and agility that GreenTech brought to the table. The partnership proved to be a win-win. GreenTech's revenue soared, and they gained recognition as a leading innovator in the industry. SolarMax strengthened its market position by offering the latest technology without the internal bottlenecks.

Alex's story illustrates how aikido principles can transform challenges into opportunities. By blending with the strengths of a larger competitor and redirecting their resources, he turned a potential adversary into a valuable ally, achieving success beyond his initial dreams.

Aikido principles offer valuable insights for entrepreneurs navigating the complex and competitive business landscape. By blending with market trends, using minimal force, maintaining balance, and turning adversaries into allies, founders can turn challenges into opportunities. The story of Alex Martinez and GreenTech Innovations serves as a testament to the power of aikido in entrepreneurship, showing that harmony and redirection can lead to innovative solutions and lasting success. Entrepreneurs who embrace these principles can not only survive but thrive in the face of adversity, creating businesses that are resilient, adaptive, and capable of achieving their visions.

CHAPTER 23

THE TRAIN RIDE WITH A MONK

THE BEGINNING

The soft hum of the train reverberated through the carriage as I settled into my seat, glancing out at the sprawling New York City skyline fading into the distance. It was early in the morning, and I was heading to Washington, DC, for a critical business meeting. As an entrepreneur struggling to raise funds, this trip felt like a last-ditch effort to secure the future of my company. I ran a small tech startup focused on developing marketing content using AI. Despite the promising potential of my ideas, I had faced countless rejections from investors. My savings were dwindling, and the weight of my employees' livelihoods rested heavily on my shoulders. Today, I was meeting with a potential investor who could change everything.

As I sighed and opened the laptop to review my presentation, the seat next to me was occupied by a man in traditional Buddhist robes. He was in his midfifties, with a serene expression and an air of tranquility that seemed almost otherworldly. He placed a small, worn-out bag under the seat and turned to me with a warm smile. "Good morning," he said in a calm, gentle voice. "My name is Tenzin. May I ask where you're headed?"

I hesitated for a moment, then replied, "I'm Sharmin, and I'm traveling to Washington, DC, for a business meeting."

"A noble endeavor," Tenzin said, nodding. "I am traveling across America to share and learn from the diverse experiences this vast land offers."

Intrigued by his calm demeanor, I asked, "Are you a monk?"

"Yes, I am a Buddhist monk from Tibet," Tenzin answered. "I believe that every journey, no matter how short or long, holds the potential for growth and learning."

THE ENCOUNTER

As the train glided smoothly through the countryside, I found myself drawn to Tenzin's peaceful presence. I couldn't help but share my struggles with him, opening up about the relentless challenges I faced as an entrepreneur. "I'm trying to revolutionize marketing technology," I explained. "But it feels like I'm constantly hitting brick walls. Investors are skeptical, resources are limited, and time is running out."

Tenzin listened intently, his eyes reflecting deep empathy. After a moment of silence, he spoke. "Sharmin, have you ever heard of the Buddhist principle of *dependent origination*?"

I shook my head. "No, I haven't."

"In Buddhism, dependent origination teaches us that all things arise in dependence upon multiple conditions. Nothing exists in isolation; everything is interconnected. This principle can be applied to your journey as an entrepreneur as well."

I leaned forward, intrigued. "How so?"

"Consider your startup," Tenzin continued. "It does not exist in isolation. It depends on the market, your team, your ideas, and the needs of your potential customers. By understanding these connections and nurturing them, you can create a harmonious balance that fosters growth and success."

LESSONS FROM THE JOURNEY

As the train journeyed on, Tenzin shared stories from his travels and the lessons he had learned. He spoke of resilience, compassion, and the importance of maintaining a balanced perspective. "In my travels, I have met many people facing various struggles," he said. "One thing I have learned is the power of mindfulness. Being present in each moment allows us to see opportunities that we might otherwise overlook."

I nodded thoughtfully. "I've been so focused on the obstacles that I might have missed some opportunities."

Tenzin smiled. "Exactly. When we focus too much on what is going wrong, we miss the chance to see what is going right. Mindfulness helps us to stay grounded and appreciate the present moment, even amid challenges." He then shared another Buddhist principle: *impermanence*. "Everything is in a constant state of change," he explained. "Both the good and the bad are temporary. By embracing this, we can remain resilient and adaptable."

I found myself reflecting on my journey as an entrepreneur. I had been so consumed by the fear of failure that I had lost sight of the progress I had made and the passion that had driven me to start my company in the first place.

ENLIGHTENMENT AND INSIGHT

As the train neared its destination, Tenzin shared one final story: In Tibet, there is a tale of a farmer who lost his horse. His neighbors came to console him, saying how unfortunate it was. But the farmer simply replied, "We'll see." The next day, the horse returned with a herd of wild horses. His neighbors congratulated him on his good fortune, but the farmer again said, "We'll see." Later, his son tried to tame one of the wild horses and broke his own leg. The neighbors expressed their sympathy, but the farmer still said, "We'll see." Soon after, soldiers came to the village to conscript young men for war, but the farmer's son was spared due to his injury. The farmer again said, "We'll see."

Tenzin paused, allowing the story to sink in. "The farmer understood that life is a series of events, each interconnected and impermanent," he continued. "What seems like a setback today may be the foundation for future success."

I felt a sense of clarity wash over me. I realized that my struggles were part of a larger journey, one that held the potential for growth and success. I thanked Tenzin for his wisdom and insights, feeling a renewed sense of hope and determination. As the train pulled into DC, I felt a profound shift within me. I was no longer burdened by the weight of my struggles but instead saw them as opportunities for growth and learning.

THE MEETING

With Tenzin's teachings fresh in my mind, I headed to my meeting with the potential investor. I walked in with a sense of calm confidence, ready to present my vision not as a desperate plea for funding but as a promising opportunity for collaboration and growth. The meeting went better than I could have hoped. The investor was impressed not only by my innovative ideas but also by my resilience and passion. They agreed to provide the funding I needed, along with strategic guidance and support.

A NEW BEGINNING

Over the next few months, my startup began to flourish. I applied the principles I had learned from Tenzin, focusing on building strong connections, staying mindful, and embracing the impermanence of my journey. I nurtured relationships with my team, ensuring that everyone felt valued and heard. I remained present in each moment, finding creative solutions to challenges as they arose. And I embraced change, understanding that each setback was an opportunity for growth.

EPILOGUE: THE POWER OF CONNECTION

As I look back, I often reflect on my encounter with Tenzin. His wisdom had not only helped me overcome my immediate struggles but had also fundamentally changed my approach to entrepreneurship and life. I decided to give back by mentoring other entrepreneurs, sharing the principles that had guided my success. I teach them about the importance of interconnectedness, mindfulness, and resilience—helping them navigate their own journeys with grace and determination.

My story is a testament to the power of connection and the profound impact that a single encounter can have. The lessons I learned from Tenzin continue to ripple out, touching the lives of countless others and creating a legacy of wisdom, compassion, and success. And so, the girl who had once struggled to raise funds for her startup found not only the financial support she needed but also a deeper understanding of what it meant to be an entrepreneur. My journey was not just about building a successful business but about growing as a person and helping others do the same. In the end, it was the principles of interconnectedness and mindfulness that had guided me to success, proving that sometimes, the most profound lessons come from the most unexpected places.

CHAPTER 24

BOOM BOOM AND HAPPY ENDINGS

Entrepreneurship is a journey fraught with challenges, exhilaration, and profound life lessons. "Boom Boom" signifies the relentless effort, the hard-hitting reality of building something from the ground up. "Happy Endings" reflect the invaluable lessons learned, the transformation, and the new beginnings that emerge from the trials.

THE SPARK

It was a warm summer evening when Max Robinson first conceived the idea for his startup. Sitting in his cramped New York apartment, the air thick with humidity, he scribbled frantically in his notebook. Max had always been a dreamer, but tonight felt different. His idea—a revolutionary fitness app that integrated personalized workout plans with mental health support—seemed like the perfect solution for a market increasingly obsessed with wellness. Max's passion was palpable. He envisioned a platform that not only helped people get fit but also supported their mental well-being. However, he knew that turning this vision into reality would require more than just enthusiasm. It would demand relentless effort—Boom Boom.

EARLY DAYS

Max quit his job the next day, diving headfirst into his startup. The initial excitement fueled sleepless nights and endless research. He pored over market studies, identified potential competitors, and outlined his business plan. His savings dwindled quickly, but he was undeterred. He believed in his idea. With no technical background, Max taught himself basic coding. He reached out to potential cofounders, eventually partnering with Lisa, a brilliant developer who shared his vision. Together, they worked tirelessly, developing the app in Lisa's garage. The long hours began to take a toll. Max lost weight, and his eyes were permanently bloodshot from lack of sleep.

THE HIGHS

After months of grueling work, the app was ready for its beta launch. The response was overwhelming. Users praised its innovative approach to fitness and mental health. Max and Lisa celebrated their initial success, feeling the rush of validation. Investors started to show interest, and they secured their first round of funding. With money in the bank, they expanded their team, bringing on board marketing experts, additional developers, and mental health professionals. The app began to gain traction, and for a moment, it seemed like the Boom Boom was paying off.

DESPERATION AND DESCENT

Success brought new challenges. The pressure to scale rapidly was immense. Investors demanded aggressive growth targets, and the once close-knit team started to fracture under the strain. Max found solace in drugs, initially just to cope with the stress, but soon it became a dependency. The once passionate and energetic entrepreneur was now a shadow of his former self, struggling to maintain focus. Max's personal life crumbled. His relationship with his girlfriend, Nicole, disintegrated as he became increasingly consumed by his work and addiction. The weight of his responsibilities felt insurmountable, leading him into a deep depression. The Boom Boom was now a relentless beat, driving him to the edge.

ROCK BOTTOM

One fateful night, Max overdosed. He was found unconscious in his apartment by Lisa, who had become increasingly concerned about his erratic behavior. The incident was a wake-up call. Max was hospitalized, and it was during his recovery that he realized the extent of his self-destruction. The board considered removing him as CEO, but Lisa and a few loyal team members stood by him. They believed in his vision and knew that MindFit could not succeed without him. However, Max needed to confront his demons and find a way to heal.

THE ROAD TO RECOVERY

Max entered rehab, determined to reclaim his life. The road to recovery was arduous. He grappled with his addiction, faced his depression head-on, and began to rebuild his physical health. In the quiet moments of introspection, he rediscovered his purpose. During his time in rehab, Max met others who had fallen into similar patterns of self-destruction. He realized that his story was not unique; many entrepreneurs struggled with the immense pressures of their journey. This insight led to a profound change in him. He resolved to not only recover for himself but to also make the app a beacon of support for those facing similar struggles.

RISING AGAIN

Returning to the company, Max was greeted with mixed emotions. Some were skeptical of his ability to lead, but he had the unwavering support of Lisa and a core group of team members. Max's transparency about his struggles and his commitment to wellness resonated deeply with them. He introduced new initiatives within the company to support mental health, ensuring that employees had access to counseling and wellness programs. This change in culture not only helped the team but also strengthened their commitment to the company's mission. Max's renewed focus and the team's collective effort led to a resurgence. They introduced new features, expanded the app's user base, and received acclaim for its holistic approach to health and wellness. The Boom Boom was no longer a destructive force but a rhythm of dedicated, purposeful work.

LESSONS LEARNED

Through his journey, Max learned invaluable lessons that reshaped his approach to entrepreneurship:

1. Balance and Well-Being: Success should not come at the cost of personal health and happiness. Maintaining a balance between work and life is crucial for sustained success.

2. Resilience and Adaptability: Challenges are inevitable, but resilience and the ability to adapt are key to overcoming them.

3. Support Systems: Building a strong support system, both personally and professionally, is essential. Isolation can lead to self-destruction, while a supportive community fosters growth.

4. Transparency and Vulnerability: Being open about struggles fosters a culture of trust and support. Vulnerability is not a weakness but a strength that connects people.

HAPPY ENDINGS AND NEW BEGINNINGS

MindFit continued to grow, becoming a leader in the wellness industry. Max's journey from the depths of despair to a renewed purpose inspired many. He began to share his story, speaking at conferences and mentoring young entrepreneurs. For Max, the Happy Ending was not just the success of his startup but the profound transformation he experienced. The Boom Boom had taught him resilience, the value of balance, and the importance of mental health. It was not the end but the beginning of a new chapter. Max's journey reflected the true essence of entrepreneurship—a path filled with highs and lows, struggles and triumphs. It was a testament to the fact that success is not just about the destination but also about the lessons learned along the way. In the end, those lessons became the foundation for new beginnings and sustained success.

BOOM BOOM AND HAPPY ENDINGS

Max stood on the stage, looking out at a sea of faces. He had been invited to deliver the keynote speech at one of the most prestigious entrepreneurship conferences. As he began to speak, he shared his story—the highs of initial success, the lows of addiction and despair, and the transformative journey that led him to where he was today. The audience was captivated. They saw in Max a reflection of their own struggles, hopes, and dreams. He spoke of the relentless effort—the Boom Boom—that every entrepreneur must put in. But he also emphasized the importance of well-being, balance, and the profound lessons that come from the journey. "For every Boom Boom," Max said, "there is a Happy Ending. But remember, that ending is not the end. It's the beginning of a new chapter, a new journey. Every struggle, every setback, is an opportunity to learn, grow, and start anew."

As applause filled the room, Max felt a deep sense of fulfillment. He had come full circle, not just in his entrepreneurial journey but in his personal growth. He knew that the path ahead would still have its challenges, but he was ready, resilient, and grounded. And so the story of Boom Boom and Happy Endings continued, with each chapter unfolding new lessons, new struggles, and new triumphs. For Max and for every entrepreneur, the journey is a testament to the enduring spirit of resilience, the power of learning, and the beauty of new beginnings.

LESSONS FROM THE JOURNEY

1. Embrace the Journey: Success is not a destination but a journey. Embrace each moment, each challenge, and each victory.

2. Prioritize Well-Being: Your health and well-being are paramount. Maintain a balance between work and personal life.

3. Build a Support System: Surround yourself with supportive people who believe in you and your vision.

4. Stay Resilient: Challenges are inevitable. Stay resilient, adapt, and learn from each setback.

5. Be Transparent and Vulnerable: Share your struggles and be open about your journey. Vulnerability fosters trust and connection.

6. Find Purpose and Passion: Let your passion drive you, and find purpose in your work. This will sustain you through the toughest times.

As you embark on your own journey, remember that each step, each struggle, and each triumph is a part of your story. Embrace the Boom Boom, cherish the Happy Endings, and always be ready for the new chapters that lie ahead.

CHAPTER 25

THE SEX WORKER WHO TAUGHT ME ENTREPRENEURSHIP

As a nineteen-year-old engineering student at a prestigious university in Bangalore, I was embarking on a journey to Pune to participate in a national engineering competition. This competition was a significant milestone in my academic career, and I was determined to make my mark. As I boarded the bus for the overnight journey, little did I know that this trip would change my life forever.

THE UNLIKELY ENCOUNTER

On the crowded bus, I found a seat next to a middle-aged woman with striking features and an air of confidence. The woman smiled warmly at me, and we exchanged pleasantries. Her name was Maya, and she was unlike anyone I had ever met. Maya exuded a sense of strength and wisdom that intrigued me.

As the bus journeyed through the night, Maya and I began to talk. She was open and candid about her life, which shocked me. Maya was a sex worker, a profession that society often looked down upon. However, Maya spoke with pride and resilience about her experiences, which captivated me. "Life has been my toughest teacher," Maya began, her voice steady. "I didn't choose this profession; it chose me. But I decided to make the best of it and turn my circumstances into opportunities."

MAYA'S STORY OF SURVIVAL

Maya's story was one of survival and resilience. She had grown up in a small village, where opportunities were scarce. At a young age, she was forced into marriage with an abusive man. After enduring years of violence and exploitation, she escaped to the city in search of a better life. However, life in the city was harsh, and she found herself with no options and no support. "I had to survive," Maya continued. "I realized that the only person who could help me was myself. I started working as a sex worker— not because I wanted to, but because it was the only way I could make money quickly."

The Entrepreneurial Spirit

Despite the hardships, Maya's entrepreneurial spirit shone through. She learned to navigate the streets, understand her clients, and manage her finances. She started saving money, investing in herself, and learning new skills. Maya's determination to rise above her circumstances was inspiring. "I treated my work like a business," Maya explained. "I built a network of clients, provided exceptional service, and ensured I managed my finances wisely. Over time, I was able to save enough to start a small business."

Lessons in Resilience

Maya's journey was not without setbacks. She faced violence, exploitation, and stigma. But she never gave up. She learned to stand up for herself and fight for her rights. Her resilience was a testament to her strength and determination. "There were times when I wanted to give up," Maya admitted. "But I reminded myself of my goals and dreams. I wanted a better life, and I was willing to fight for it. Every setback was a lesson, and I used those lessons to become stronger."

The Turning Point

One night, Maya was brutally assaulted by a client. The incident left her physically and emotionally scarred. But it also became a turning point in her life. She realized that she needed to find a way out of the sex trade and pursue her dreams of entrepreneurship. "I was at my lowest point," Maya recalled. "But I refused to let that incident define me. I decided to take control of my life and focus on my dreams."

Building a Business

Maya used her savings to start a small tailoring business. She had always been good with her hands and had a passion for fashion. She took courses, learned new skills, and built a network of clients. Her business began to grow, and she was able to leave the sex trade behind. "I poured my heart and soul into my business," Maya said with pride. "I learned to market my products, manage my finances, and build relationships with my clients. It wasn't easy, but I was determined to succeed."

As I listened to Maya's story, I was deeply moved. Maya's resilience and entrepreneurial spirit inspired me. I realized that I, too, had the power to overcome challenges and pursue my dreams. "Maya, your story is incredible," I said, my eyes shining with admiration. "You've taught me so much about resilience and never giving up. I want to be an entrepreneur someday, and your journey has given me the courage to pursue my dreams."

The Power of Influence

Maya's ability to influence others was one of her greatest strengths. She had learned to build trust, communicate effectively, and inspire others. These skills were essential in her journey as an entrepreneur. "Sharmin, remember that the power to influence others is key to success in entrepreneurship," Maya advised. "Whether it's convincing investors to fund your idea, persuading customers to buy your product, or motivating your team, the ability to influence and inspire others is crucial."

Diverse Revenue Streams

Maya also taught me the importance of diversifying revenue streams. In her tailoring business, Maya offered a range of products and services, ensuring that she was not reliant on a single source of income. "Always look for multiple ways to make money," Maya advised. "Diversifying your revenue streams not only increases your income but also reduces your risk."

The Journey to Pune

As the bus neared Pune, I felt a sense of excitement and determination. Maya's story had given me a new perspective on life and entrepreneurship. I was ready to face the competition with confidence and pursue my dreams of becoming an entrepreneur. "Maya, thank you for sharing your story with me," I said, my voice filled with gratitude. "You've taught me so much about resilience, determination, and the power of entrepreneurship. I will carry these lessons with me always."

The Competition

I arrived at the competition with a newfound sense of purpose. I presented my project with confidence and passion, drawing inspiration from Maya's story. My hard work and determination paid off, and I won the competition. As I stood on the stage, holding my trophy, I thought of Maya and the incredible journey we had shared. I knew that this was just the beginning of my entrepreneurial journey.

CHAPTER 26

THE POWER OF THE PODIUM: WHY ENTREPRENEURS SHOULD EMBRACE KEYNOTE SPEAKING

Keynote speaking is often seen as a prestigious and influential platform, where leaders and experts share their insights and experiences with a wide audience. For entrepreneurs, becoming a keynote speaker is not just about the honor of standing on a stage; it's about leveraging that stage to drive significant benefits for their company, personal growth, and broader impact. Here's why every entrepreneur should consider becoming a keynote speaker and how it can transform their business and life.

THE IMPORTANCE OF KEYNOTE SPEAKING FOR ENTREPRENEURS

❶ Establishing Authority and Credibility

As an entrepreneur, credibility and authority in your industry are crucial. Keynote speaking allows you to establish yourself as an expert and thought leader. When you deliver a compelling keynote, you demonstrate your knowledge, experience, and vision to a large audience, which helps build trust and credibility.

EXAMPLE Consider Steve Jobs, whose keynote addresses at Apple events were legendary. His presentations not only introduced groundbreaking products but also solidified his reputation as a visionary leader in technology.

❷ Expanding Your Reach and Influence

Keynote speaking offers a platform to reach a broader audience beyond your immediate network. By speaking at conferences, industry events, and seminars, you can connect with potential clients, partners, investors, and other stakeholders who can help propel your business forward.

EXAMPLE Sarah Blakely, the founder of Spanx, frequently shares her entrepreneurial journey and insights through keynote speeches, inspiring a wide audience and expanding her influence far beyond the fashion industry.

❸ Driving Brand Awareness and Loyalty

When you speak at events, you're not just representing yourself; you're representing your brand. Keynote speaking is an excellent way to enhance brand awareness and build loyalty. By sharing your company's mission, values, and success stories, you create a deeper connection with your audience, turning them into brand advocates.

EXAMPLE Tony Robbins, through his motivational speaking, has built a massive following and a powerful brand that extends into various business ventures, from personal development to financial services.

❹ Attracting Investment and Partnership Opportunities

Investors and potential partners often attend industry conferences and events to discover new opportunities. A well-delivered keynote can attract their attention and interest. By articulating your vision and showcasing your company's potential, you can open doors to investment and strategic partnerships.

EXAMPLE: Elon Musk has used keynote speaking at events like Tesla's shareholder meetings and product launches to attract investors and build partnerships that drive his companies forward.

❺ Acquiring New Clients

Keynote speaking can be a powerful lead generation tool. When you present valuable insights and solutions to your audience's challenges, you position yourself and your company as the go-to resource. This can lead to direct inquiries and new client acquisitions.

EXAMPLE: Gary Vaynerchuk, through his energetic keynote speeches, attracts businesses and entrepreneurs seeking marketing expertise, leading to new clients for his digital agency, VaynerMedia.

❻ Hiring Top Talent

A company's success depends heavily on its ability to attract and retain top talent. Keynote speaking allows you to showcase your company culture, values, and vision, making it more attractive to potential employees. When talented individuals see a passionate and inspiring leader, they are more likely to want to join your team.

EXAMPLE Sheryl Sandberg, former COO of Facebook, often speaks at conferences about leadership and company culture, helping attract and retain some of the best talent in the industry.

7 Personal and Professional Growth

Keynote speaking contributes significantly to personal and professional development. Preparing and delivering a keynote requires deep introspection, clarity of thought, and effective communication skills. This process helps you refine your ideas, improve your public speaking abilities, and gain confidence.

EXAMPLE Brené Brown, originally an academic researcher, grew personally and professionally by sharing her work on vulnerability and courage through keynote speeches, which led to bestselling books and a global following.

8 Leaving a Legacy

Keynote speaking is a way to leave a lasting impact. By sharing your journey, lessons learned, and vision for the future, you can inspire and influence the next generation of entrepreneurs. Your words can leave a legacy that transcends your immediate business achievements.

EXAMPLE Richard Branson, through his speeches and writings, has inspired countless entrepreneurs to pursue their dreams and think big, leaving a legacy of innovation and adventure.

HOW TO BECOME A SUCCESSFUL KEYNOTE SPEAKER

❶ Identify Your Unique Message

To become a successful keynote speaker, you need to identify what sets you apart. What unique experiences, insights, or perspectives can you offer? Focus on your personal journey, challenges overcome, and lessons learned. Authenticity and originality are key to resonating with your audience.

EXAMPLE Blake Mycoskie, founder of TOMS Shoes, shares his unique story of creating a socially responsible business, inspiring others to consider the impact of their entrepreneurial ventures.

❷ Develop Compelling Content

Your content should be engaging, informative, and actionable. Use storytelling to connect with your audience emotionally. Incorporate real-life examples, case studies, and practical advice that your audience can apply. Ensure your message is clear, concise, and aligned with the event's theme and audience interests.

EXAMPLE Simon Sinek's keynote speeches on leadership and the power of "Why" are compelling because they combine storytelling with practical insights and a clear, memorable message.

❸ Hone Your Public Speaking Skills

Effective public speaking is a skill you can develop with practice. Join public speaking groups like Toastmasters, take speaking courses, and seek opportunities to practice. Focus on improving your delivery, body language, and ability to engage with your audience.

EXAMPLE Barack Obama is renowned for his eloquent and impactful speeches, a skill honed through years of practice and public speaking engagements.

❹ Build Your Speaking Portfolio

Start by speaking at smaller events, workshops, or webinars to build your portfolio. Collect testimonials, video recordings, and feedback to showcase your speaking abilities. As you gain experience, you can apply to speak at larger conferences and industry events.

EXAMPLE Neil Patel, a digital marketing expert, built his speaking portfolio by starting with small marketing events and gradually progressing to major industry conferences.

❺ Leverage Social Media and Content Marketing

Use social media and content marketing to promote your keynote speaking. Share snippets of your speeches, behind-the-scenes preparation, and audience feedback on platforms like LinkedIn, X, and YouTube. Create blog posts, articles, and podcasts to reach a broader audience.

EXAMPLE Tim Ferriss leverages his blog, podcast, and social media to share insights from his speeches and connect with a global audience, further establishing his authority and influence.

❻ Network and Seek Speaking Opportunities

Actively seek out speaking opportunities by networking with event organizers, joining industry associations, and participating in speaking bureaus. Attend conferences and engage with other speakers to learn about upcoming events and opportunities.

EXAMPLE Arianna Huffington, through her extensive network and participation in industry events, secures numerous speaking engagements where she shares her insights on leadership, well-being, and media.

❼ Continuously Improve and Adapt

The best keynote speakers continuously improve their skills and adapt to changing trends and audience preferences. Seek feedback after each speaking engagement, reflect on what worked and what didn't, and make necessary adjustments. Stay updated on industry trends, and incorporate relevant topics into your speeches.

EXAMPLE Tony Hsieh, former CEO of Zappos, continuously refined his speeches on company culture and customer service by incorporating new insights and audience feedback.

THE TRANSFORMATIONAL IMPACT OF KEYNOTE SPEAKING

Keynote speaking can have a transformational impact on an entrepreneur's business and life. Here's how:

❶ Elevating Your Company's Profile

By speaking at prominent events, you elevate your company's profile. You create visibility and awareness, attracting media coverage and positioning your company as an industry leader.

EXAMPLE Marc Benioff, founder and CEO of Salesforce, uses keynote speaking at events like Dreamforce to elevate Salesforce's profile, attracting customers, partners, and media attention.

❷ Creating Valuable Connections

Keynote speaking allows you to connect with other industry leaders, potential clients, partners, and investors. These connections can lead to valuable collaborations, business opportunities, and strategic partnerships.

EXAMPLE Reid Hoffman, cofounder of LinkedIn, has built a vast network of connections through keynote speaking, leading to strategic partnerships and investment opportunities.

❸ Inspiring and Motivating Others

As a keynote speaker, you have the power to inspire and motivate others. Your story and insights can influence aspiring entrepreneurs, business leaders, and professionals, encouraging them to pursue their goals and dreams.

EXAMPLE Oprah Winfrey inspires millions by sharing her journey of overcoming adversity and achieving success, motivating others to follow their dreams.

❹ Driving Business Growth

Keynote speaking can directly drive business growth by attracting new clients, customers, and investors. By showcasing your expertise and vision, you create interest and demand for your products or services.

EXAMPLE Steve Wozniak, cofounder of Apple, uses keynote speaking to attract new clients and partnerships for his ventures, driving business growth.

5 Enhancing Your Personal Brand

Your personal brand is a reflection of your reputation and influence. Keynote speaking enhances your personal brand by positioning you as an expert and thought leader. A strong personal brand can open doors to new opportunities and ventures.

EXAMPLE: Richard Branson's personal brand as an adventurous and innovative entrepreneur is reinforced through his keynote speeches, enhancing his influence and attracting new opportunities.

6 Leaving a Legacy

Keynote speaking allows you to leave a legacy. Your words and insights can impact generations, inspiring future entrepreneurs and leaders. By sharing your journey and lessons learned, you contribute to the collective knowledge and inspire positive change.

CHAPTER 27

BITCH, STOP! PLEASE....: BURNOUT–THE UNSEEN BATTLE

I believe in work, hard work, and long hours of work. Men do not breakdown from overwork, but from worry and dissipation

—CHARLES EVANS HUGHES

I stood at the balcony of my penthouse apartment, gazing at the glittering cityscape of San Francisco. The skyline, bathed in the glow of countless lights, seemed to mirror my elation. Just hours ago, I had secured a $200 million funding commitment, the final step before my startup would go public. The realization was surreal. Inside, my cofounder and best friend, Raj, poured champagne into crystal flutes. "To us!" he toasted, his eyes gleaming with pride.

"To us!" I echoed, clinking my glass against his. As the bubbles danced on my tongue, I felt a surge of accomplishment. This was the culmination of four and a half years of relentless hard work, sleepless nights, and countless sacrifices. We had turned a nascent idea into a tech powerhouse poised to revolutionize the industry. The celebration continued late into the night, with laughter and reminiscences filling the air. But as Raj left and the apartment fell silent, a strange weariness settled over me. I had been pushing myself to the limit for so long that I barely remembered what it felt like to rest.

THE SILENT STRUGGLE

Weeks passed in a whirlwind of meetings, press conferences, and endless preparations for the next big thing. My schedule was packed from dawn until late into the night. Despite the excitement, I felt a persistent undercurrent of anxiety. I often found myself staring blankly at the computer screen, my heart pounding in my chest. My lifestyle had become a blur of coffee-fueled mornings and takeout dinners. Sleep was a luxury I could no longer afford, and meals were often skipped or replaced by energy bars. The pressure to succeed was immense, and there was no room for weakness. One night, as I reviewed the final details of our next meeting, a sharp pain shot through my chest. I ignored it, attributing it to stress and fatigue. But the pain persisted, accompanied by a tightness that made it hard to breathe. I pressed a hand to my chest, trying to ease the discomfort away.

THE COLLAPSE

It was 3:00 a.m. when I awoke with a jolt. The pain in my chest had intensified, radiating down my left arm. My vision blurred, and a cold sweat broke out on my forehead. Panic seized me as I realized something was seriously wrong. My mind raced. I was alone in the apartment, with no one to help. Summoning all my strength, I reached for my phone and dialed 911. The operator's voice was calm and reassuring, but I could barely focus on the words. "I . . . I think I'm having a heart attack," I managed to gasp.

"Stay on the line, ma'am. Help is on the way," the operator said. I struggled to remain conscious, each second feeling like an eternity. I could hear the distant wail of sirens growing louder. The world around me dimmed, and I felt myself slipping away.

THE AFTERMATH

When I regained consciousness, I was in a hospital bed, surrounded by the rhythmic beeping of machines. I blinked, disoriented, as a nurse approached. "You're awake. That's good," the nurse said, her voice gentle. "You had a cardiac arrest. The doctors are monitoring you closely."

A wave of disbelief washed over me. Cardiac arrest? At thirty-four? How could this have happened? I tried to sit up, but a sharp pain in my chest forced me to lie back down. A few hours later, Dr. Patel, a cardiologist, entered the room. He had a stern yet compassionate expression. "Sharmin, you had a minor cardiac arrest," he explained. "Your body has been under immense stress, and your lifestyle has taken a serious toll on your heart. If you continue like this, you won't live long."

I stared at him, my mind reeling. The gravity of his words sunk in, and tears welled up in my eyes. I had been so consumed by my drive for success that I had ignored the warning signs my body had been sending. "You need to make some serious changes," Dr. Patel continued. "Rest, proper nutrition, and a balanced lifestyle are essential. I recommend you take a break from work and focus on your health."

THE DECISION

Back at my apartment, I felt a profound sense of emptiness. The very space that had once symbolized my success now felt like a cage. I looked at the stacks of paperwork, the awards, and the framed articles heralding my achievements. None of it seemed to matter anymore. Raj visited, concern etched on his face. "Sharmin, you need to prioritize your health. The company can't function without you, but it won't matter if you're not here." I knew he was right. The realization hit me like a ton of bricks: I needed to step back, for my own sake.

That evening, I drafted a letter to the board, announcing my decision to take a leave of absence and eventually exit the company. The next morning, I called a meeting with my executive team. As I spoke, my voice steady but emotional, I saw a mixture of shock and understanding on their faces. "I need to take care of myself," I said, concluding my speech. "Raj will lead the company in my absence. I trust you all to continue our vision and take it to new heights."

THE HEALING JOURNEY

Leaving the company was both a relief and a heartache. I felt like I was abandoning my child, but I knew it was necessary. I decided to take a year off, to disconnect from the relentless pace of the business world and reconnect with myself. My first few weeks of freedom were challenging. I had to unlearn the habits of constant work and learn to embrace rest. Simple activities like cooking a healthy meal or taking a walk in the park felt foreign but slowly became a source of joy. I traveled to quiet retreats, practiced meditation, and reconnected with old friends and family. For the first time in years, I felt truly alive. My health improved, and the spark of life returned to my eyes. One evening, while watching the sunset on a serene beach, I reflected on my journey. The cardiac arrest had been a wake-up call, forcing me to reevaluate my priorities. Success was important, but not at the cost of my health and well-being.

A NEW BEGINNING

A year later, I returned to San Francisco with a renewed sense of purpose. I had decided to start a new venture, one that focused on promoting wellness and balance for entrepreneurs. I wanted to share my story and help others avoid the pitfalls I had encountered. With Raj's support, I launched the Sharmin Ali Foundation for Entrepreneurs (SAFE), a platform dedicated to providing resources, coaching, and community for entrepreneurs looking to balance success with well-being, to help them navigate mental health challenges at work.

My experience gave me a unique perspective, and my passion for the cause resonated with many. My journey had come full circle. I had achieved incredible success, faced a life-threatening challenge, and emerged stronger and wiser. I realized that true success wasn't just about financial achievements but also about living a healthy, balanced, and fulfilling life. As I looked out at the city once more, I felt a deep sense of peace. I had found my true calling, and this time, I was determined to do it right.

CHAPTER 28

PILATES

I stared at my reflection in the mirror, hardly recognizing the woman I had become. At thirty-five, I was supposed to be at the peak of my life and career. Instead, I was grappling with the aftermath of a cardiac arrest that had struck me down at thirty-four, and a diagnosis of depression that had followed soon after. The stress of running my startup had taken a heavy toll on my body and mind, leaving me feeling defeated and exhausted. One afternoon, while scrolling aimlessly through social media, I stumbled upon a post about Pilates. Intrigued by the idea of a low-impact exercise that promised to strengthen both body and mind, I decided to give it a try. I signed up for a class at a nearby studio, determined to find a way to reclaim my health and sanity.

The studio was a serene space, filled with natural light and the soothing scent of lavender. On my first day, I met my trainer, Keiry, a thirty-eight-year-old woman with an infectious enthusiasm for life and an impressive knowledge of Pilates. "Welcome, Sharmin," Keiry greeted me warmly. "Pilates is about finding balance and strength from within. Let's start your journey."

The first few sessions were challenging. My body felt stiff and uncooperative, but Keiry's patience and encouragement kept me going. Keiry had a way of making each exercise feel like a step toward healing rather than a punishing workout. "Remember, Sharmin," Keiry would say, "Pilates is about connecting with your body. Listen to it, respect it, and you'll be amazed at what it can do." As the weeks passed, I began to notice changes. My posture improved, and the persistent ache in my back started to ease. More importantly, the fog of depression began to lift. I started to feel a spark of energy that I hadn't felt in a long time.

One day, after a particularly grueling session, I collapsed onto my mat, laughing at my own exhaustion. Keiry sat beside me, a knowing smile on her face. "You're doing great, Sharmin. Remember, this is not just about losing weight or building muscles. It's about finding your inner strength. You have to believe in yourself."

I took those words to heart. I pushed myself harder, not just in the studio but in life. I began to see my challenges not as insurmountable obstacles but as opportunities to grow and learn. Keiry's lessons extended beyond the physical realm. During our sessions, we often talked about life, struggles, and resilience. Keiry shared her own story of overcoming adversity—how she had left an unfulfilling corporate job to pursue her passion for Pilates, and how that decision had transformed her life. "You see, Sharmin," Keiry said one day, "we all have our battles. But it's how we face them that defines us. Pilates taught me to be present, to focus on what I can control, and to let go of what I can't."

These conversations were as therapeutic as the exercises themselves. I found myself opening up about my fears and insecurities, about the pressure I felt as an entrepreneur, and the toll it had taken on my health. Keiry listened with empathy and offered wisdom that resonated deeply with me. "Running a business is like doing Pilates," she said. "It requires balance, focus, and strength. But most importantly, it requires you to be kind to yourself. You can't pour from an empty cup, Sharmin. Take care of yourself first."

As I continued my Pilates journey, I started to see remarkable changes. In just two months, I lost twenty pounds. But more than that, I gained a renewed sense of self-worth and confidence. The depression that had once clouded my mind began to dissipate, replaced by a clarity and determination I hadn't felt in years. One evening, after a particularly intense session, I sat with Keiry in the quiet studio, reflecting on my progress. "You've come a long way, Sharmin," Keiry said, her eyes filled with pride. "Remember, this journey is yours. Celebrate your successes, learn from your setbacks, and keep moving forward."

I nodded, feeling a surge of gratitude for Keiry and the transformation Pilates had brought into my life. I realized that working out had become more than just a physical activity; it was a form of therapy, a way to navigate the challenges of life with grace and resilience. Armed with newfound strength and clarity, I began to approach my life with a different mindset. I prioritized my well-being, knowing that my health was the foundation of my success. It was about discovering the power of resilience, the importance of self-care, and the incredible impact that one person's support and encouragement can have on another's life. Through my experience, I learned that working out was indeed the best medicine for an entrepreneur going through a difficult time. It taught me to face my challenges head-on, to find strength in the face of adversity, and to never underestimate the power of a healthy mind and body.

CHAPTER 29

LOVE THE SMELL OF NAPALM IN THE MORNING: EMBRACING THE CHAOS OF ENTREPRENEURSHIP

In the world of entrepreneurship, uncertainty and unpredictability are as common as coffee breaks and board meetings. For many, these elements might seem like obstacles to overcome, but for successful entrepreneurs, they are essential ingredients in the recipe for success. The metaphorical "napalm" in this context signifies the intense, often overwhelming challenges faced on a daily basis. It represents the chaos, risks, and unpredictability inherent in building a startup. Embracing and even reveling in this chaos can be the key to not just surviving but thriving on the entrepreneurial battlefield. Let us explore the concept of "loving the smell of napalm in the morning," that memorable line from the controversial war film *Apocalypse Now*, as a metaphor for accepting and even enjoying the inherent uncertainty of entrepreneurship. We'll dive into how entrepreneurs can transform these challenges into opportunities, using real-life examples and practical strategies to navigate and conquer the chaos.

THE NATURE OF NAPALM IN ENTREPRENEURSHIP

Uncertainty as the New Normal

Napalm, a highly flammable liquid used in warfare, is synonymous with death, destruction, and chaos. In the realm of entrepreneurship, the term represents the unpredictable and tumultuous nature of the startup journey. From fluctuating markets to sudden changes in consumer behavior, uncertainty is a constant companion. For entrepreneurs, uncertainty manifests in various forms:

1. **Market Volatility:** Rapid changes in market conditions can impact product demand and business viability.

2. **Funding Challenges:** Securing investment can be unpredictable, with many startups facing rejections before finding the right backers.

3. **Operational Hiccups:** Unexpected issues with supply chains, technology failures, or team dynamics can arise at any moment.

4. **Competitive Pressures:** The constant threat of new competitors and evolving industry trends keeps entrepreneurs on their toes.

EMBRACING THE CHAOS

Accepting and even embracing this chaos can be liberating. Instead of viewing uncertainty as a hindrance, successful entrepreneurs learn to see it as an opportunity for innovation and growth. This mindset shift is crucial for thriving in the unpredictable world of startups.

The Benefits of Embracing Uncertainty

⚙ FOSTERING INNOVATION

Uncertainty forces entrepreneurs to think creatively and adapt quickly. When faced with unpredictable circumstances, startups are often pushed to innovate, finding new solutions and approaches that might not have been considered in a more stable environment.

EXAMPLE During the COVID-19 pandemic, many businesses were forced to pivot rapidly. Restaurants developed innovative delivery models, fitness studios launched virtual classes, and companies embraced remote work solutions. These adaptations led to new business models and opportunities that might not have emerged under normal circumstances.

⚙ DEVELOPING RESILIENCE

Regularly navigating uncertainty builds resilience. Entrepreneurs who thrive in chaotic environments develop robust mental and emotional fortitude, allowing them to handle future challenges with greater ease.

EXAMPLE Elon Musk's journey with Tesla and SpaceX is a testament to resilience. Musk faced numerous setbacks, including production delays and financial struggles, but his ability to persevere through these challenges has been key to his companies' success.

⚙ ENHANCING AGILITY

In a volatile market, agility is a crucial advantage. Startups that are adaptable and quick to pivot can respond to changing conditions more effectively than larger, more rigid organizations.

EXAMPLE Netflix's transition from DVD rentals to streaming services is a prime example of agility. The company recognized shifting consumer preferences and adapted its business model accordingly, staying ahead of competitors and dominating the entertainment industry.

Strategies for Embracing and Leveraging Uncertainty

❶ CULTIVATE A GROWTH MINDSET

A growth mindset is essential for thriving in the face of uncertainty. Entrepreneurs with a growth mindset view challenges as opportunities for learning and improvement, rather than as threats.

PRACTICAL TIP Regularly reflect on past challenges and how they contributed to your growth. This can help reinforce the idea that uncertainty leads to personal and professional development.

❷ BUILD A STRONG SUPPORT NETWORK

Having a reliable support network can provide guidance and reassurance during tumultuous times. Surround yourself with mentors, advisors, and peers who can offer valuable insights and encouragement.

PRACTICAL TIP Join entrepreneurial communities, attend networking events, and seek out mentorship programs to build a robust support system.

❸ IMPLEMENT AGILE PRACTICES

Agile methodologies, commonly used in software development, emphasize flexibility and iterative progress. Applying agile principles to your business operations can help you adapt quickly to changes and continuously improve your strategies.

PRACTICAL TIP: Break down projects into smaller, manageable tasks and regularly review and adjust your approach based on feedback and results.

4 MAINTAIN FINANCIAL FLEXIBILITY

Unpredictable financial situations are common in startups. Maintaining a financial cushion and being prepared for unexpected expenses can help you navigate periods of uncertainty without derailing your business.

PRACTICAL TIP: Build an emergency fund and regularly review your financial projections. Explore alternative funding options, such as lines of credit or strategic partnerships, to enhance financial flexibility.

5 FOCUS ON CUSTOMER FEEDBACK

Customer feedback is a valuable source of information that can guide your business decisions. By actively seeking and responding to feedback, you can better understand market needs and adjust your strategies accordingly.

PRACTICAL TIP: Implement regular customer surveys, engage with your audience on social media, and analyze feedback to inform product development and marketing efforts.

Real-Life Examples of Embracing Uncertainty

❶ AMAZON'S EVOLUTION

Amazon's journey from an online bookstore to a global e-commerce and technology giant exemplifies the power of embracing uncertainty. Jeff Bezos continuously adapted the company's strategy, experimenting with new business models and technologies. Amazon's success is a result of its willingness to take risks and innovate in the face of uncertainty.

❷ AIRBNB'S RESILIENCE

Airbnb's response to the COVID-19 pandemic highlights the benefits of embracing uncertainty. The company faced a dramatic decline in travel but quickly pivoted to focus on long-term stays and local experiences. This adaptability allowed Airbnb to navigate the crisis and emerge stronger.

❸ SLACK'S TRANSFORMATION

Slack's initial failure as a gaming company was a turning point for the team. Recognizing the potential of their internal communication tool, they pivoted to focus on developing Slack as a productivity platform. This shift in strategy allowed them to capitalize on market needs and achieve significant success.

The Psychological Impact of Embracing Uncertainty

❶ REDUCING STRESS AND ANXIETY

Accepting uncertainty can alleviate the stress and anxiety associated with trying to control every aspect of your business. By focusing on what you can control and adapting to what you can't, you can maintain a healthy mental state.

PRACTICAL TIP: Practice mindfulness and stress-reduction techniques to manage anxiety and maintain a balanced perspective.

❷ ENHANCING CREATIVITY

Embracing uncertainty can foster a more creative mindset. When you're not bound by rigid expectations or fear of failure, you're more likely to explore innovative solutions and take calculated risks.

PRACTICAL TIP: Create an environment that encourages experimentation and creative thinking. Allow yourself and your team to explore new ideas without an expectation of immediate success or a fear of failure.

❸ BUILDING CONFIDENCE

Successfully navigating uncertainty can build confidence in your ability to handle challenges. Each success, no matter how small, reinforces a belief in your capabilities and prepares you for future obstacles.

PRACTICAL TIP: Celebrate your achievements and milestones, no matter how minor. Recognizing your progress can boost confidence and motivation.

On the entrepreneurial battlefield, "loving the smell of napalm in the morning" signifies embracing and thriving in the chaos and uncertainty that come with building a startup. By accepting the unpredictability of the entrepreneurial journey and viewing challenges as opportunities for growth, entrepreneurs can transform obstacles into stepping stones for success.

Manifesting a startup requires more than just dreaming about success—it requires a proactive approach to managing and leveraging uncertainty. By cultivating a growth mindset, building a strong support network, implementing agile practices, maintaining financial flexibility, and focusing on customer feedback, entrepreneurs can navigate the unpredictable terrain of entrepreneurship with confidence and resilience.

As you embark on your entrepreneurial journey, remember that uncertainty is not an enemy but a powerful ally. Embrace the chaos, revel in the challenges, and let the smell of napalm inspire you to push beyond your limits. In doing so, you'll discover that the path to success is not just about overcoming obstacles but about thriving in the face of them. So rise to the challenge, love the chaos, and let the smell of napalm guide you to new heights in your entrepreneurial journey. Your willingness to embrace uncertainty and turn it into opportunity will set you apart and pave the way for extraordinary success.

CHAPTER 30

THE ART OF WAR

ATTACKING DURING A TRUCE: ENTREPRENEURIAL WAR TACTICS

In the world of entrepreneurship, there are no permanent allies or enemies, only interests that align or diverge at various points in time. The business landscape is often likened to a battlefield, where Sun Tzu's classic text *The Art of War* might apply. Strategies, tactics, and maneuvers determine success or failure. Sometimes, just as in ancient wars, the notion of a truce is merely a strategic pause rather than an absolute peace. This chapter will delve into the metaphor of attacking during a truce in war, and its relevance to entrepreneurship, drawing on lessons from the *Mahabharata*, the Bhagavad Gita, the Quran, and other mythologies to illustrate why sometimes breaking a truce is necessary for survival and success.

A truce in war signifies a temporary cessation of hostilities, a moment of respite for both sides to regroup, recover, and perhaps renegotiate terms. However, in the ruthless world of warfare, truces are often fragile and can be broken when one side perceives an advantage. The same applies to the competitive business environment, where temporary alliances or ceasefires may be necessary but are not inviolable.

255

HISTORICAL AND MYTHOLOGICAL CONTEXT

In many historical and mythological accounts, truces have been broken to achieve strategic advantages. These stories provide valuable insights into the nature of conflict and the moral complexities of leadership and decision-making.

Example from the *Mahabharata*

The *Mahabharata*, one of India's greatest epics, provides profound lessons in strategy and ethics. One such example involves the truce between the Pandavas and the Kauravas. During the Kurukshetra War, on the thirteenth day, Arjuna's son, Abhimanyu, was caught inside the Chakravyuha (a military formation) created by the Kauravas. Despite the rules of war (Dharma Yuddha) that prohibited multiple warriors attacking a single warrior, the Kauravas broke the truce and attacked Abhimanyu en masse, leading to his tragic death. From an entrepreneurial perspective, this incident highlights that the battlefield (market) does not always adhere to rules and ethics when the stakes are high. While Abhimanyu's death was tragic, it was a stark reminder that in the ruthless quest for dominance, fairness can sometimes be a casualty.

Lessons from the Bhagavad Gita

The Bhagavad Gita, a philosophical dialogue between Prince Arjuna and the god Krishna, offers timeless wisdom on duty, righteousness, and strategic action. When Arjuna hesitates to fight in the Kurukshetra War, Krishna advises him on the importance of fulfilling one's duty without attachment to the results. Krishna emphasizes that inaction is also a form of action, and sometimes, decisive and seemingly harsh actions are necessary to restore balance and justice. In the entrepreneurial context, this translates to the necessity of making tough decisions, including breaking temporary truces or alliances if they hinder your ultimate mission. An entrepreneur must be willing to take bold steps to secure their business's future, even if it means facing ethical dilemmas.

THE STRATEGIC VALUE OF BREAKING A TRUCE

In business, as in war, a truce can be a double-edged sword. It offers a chance to regroup and strategize but can also lull one into a false sense of security. Understanding when to uphold or break a truce is a critical skill for entrepreneurs.

Maintaining a Competitive Advantage

The primary goal of any business is to maintain a competitive advantage. Sometimes, this requires taking actions that are not immediately obvious or conventional. A temporary truce with a competitor might provide short-term stability, but if an opportunity arises to gain a significant advantage, breaking that truce could be justified. Consider the tech industry, where companies often collaborate on standards and technologies while fiercely competing in the market. An example is the collaboration between Apple and Google on certain technologies, even though they are direct competitors in the smartphone market. If one company finds an innovative leap that could disrupt the market, they might choose to act unilaterally despite any ongoing collaboration.

The Element of Surprise

One of the most effective strategies in warfare is the element of surprise. In entrepreneurship, catching competitors off guard by launching a new product, entering a new market, or executing a strategic partnership can provide a significant advantage. An example from history is the Trojan Horse strategy from Greek mythology. The Greeks pretended to abandon their siege of Troy, leaving behind a wooden horse as a supposed peace offering. The Trojans brought the horse inside their city walls, only to find it filled with Greek soldiers who opened the gates to the city for the returning Greek army, leading to Troy's downfall. In the business world, a similar strategy can be employed by creating a false sense of security before launching a disruptive innovation. This tactic, while ruthless, can lead to significant breakthroughs and market dominance.

Ethical Considerations

Breaking a truce is fraught with ethical considerations. The Quran, for example, emphasizes the importance of honoring treaties and agreements. Surah An-Nahl (16:91) states, "And fulfill the covenant of Allah when you have taken it, and do not break oaths after their confirmation while you have made Allah, over you, a witness. Indeed, Allah knows what you do." However, even in the Quran, there are provisions for breaking treaties under certain circumstances, especially when the other party has already violated the terms. This underscores the importance of context and intent in ethical decision-making. For entrepreneurs, this means carefully weighing the consequences of breaking a truce. If the move is justified by the behavior of the other party or by the necessity to protect the business's survival and growth, it might be ethically permissible.

EXAMPLES FROM MODERN ENTREPRENEURSHIP

Apple versus Microsoft

The rivalry between Apple and Microsoft is a classic example of strategic truces and rivalries. In the 1990s, both companies were fierce competitors in the personal computing market. However, in 1997, Apple was on the brink of bankruptcy, and Microsoft invested $150 million in Apple, effectively providing a lifeline. This truce was strategic for both parties: Apple gained much-needed financial stability, while Microsoft ensured that it had a competitor to prevent monopoly accusations. However, the truce did not mean an end to their rivalry. Both companies continued to compete aggressively in other areas, with Apple eventually becoming one of the most valuable companies in the world through innovations like the iPhone.

Netflix and Blockbuster

Another example is the competition between Netflix and Block-buster. In the early 2000s, Blockbuster had the opportunity to purchase Netflix for $50 million but chose not to. Netflix, a fledgling company at the time, continued to innovate and eventually disrupted Blockbuster's business model entirely. Blockbuster's failure to recognize the strategic value of a truce (or acquisition in this case) led to its downfall. Meanwhile, Netflix's aggressive and innovative approach ensured its survival and dominance in the streaming industry.

PRACTICAL GUIDELINES FOR ENTREPRENEURS

Assessing the Truce

Before deciding to break a truce, entrepreneurs must conduct a thorough assessment. This involves understanding the strategic value of the truce, the potential gains from breaking it, and the risks involved. Here are some questions to consider:

1. What is the long-term impact of maintaining or breaking the truce?

2. How will stakeholders—including customers, employees, and partners—react?

3. What are the ethical implications, and how will they affect the company's reputation?

Planning the Attack

If the decision is made to break the truce, meticulous planning is essential. This includes the following:

1. Developing a clear strategy and timeline for the action.

2. Ensuring that resources are in place to support the initiative.

3. Communicating effectively with internal teams to align efforts.

Managing the Aftermath

Breaking a truce will have repercussions. Entrepreneurs must be prepared to manage the aftermath by doing these things:

1. Addressing any backlash from stakeholders.

2. Reinforcing the company's core values and mission.

3. Continuously monitoring and adjusting strategies to navigate the new competitive landscape.

Learning and Adapting

The business environment is dynamic, and entrepreneurs must

remain agile. Learning from both successes and failures is crucial. Reflecting on past decisions and adapting strategies accordingly will help in navigating future challenges.

Attacking during a truce, while controversial, can be a necessary strategy in the high-stakes world of entrepreneurship. The lessons from the *Mahabharata*, the Bhagavad Gita, the Quran, and modern business examples all illustrate that the path to success is rarely straightforward. It involves tough decisions, ethical dilemmas, and strategic maneuvers. Entrepreneurs must navigate these complexities with wisdom, agility, and a keen understanding of their competitive landscape. By embracing the metaphor of war, they can develop strategies that not only ensure survival but also drive innovation and growth. Remember, on the ever-evolving battlefield of business, sometimes the bold move of breaking a truce is necessary to achieve greatness.

CHAPTER 31

VANITY IS MY FAVORITE SIN

Vanity is often seen as a negative trait, associated with excessive pride in one's appearance or achievements. However, in the realm of entrepreneurship, vanity can be transformed into a powerful tool, particularly in marketing and public relations (PR). When harnessed correctly, vanity can drive an entrepreneur to create a compelling personal brand, engage with a global audience, and position their company for unparalleled success. Let us explore why vanity should be an entrepreneur's favorite sin, emphasizing the importance of PR and marketing, and detailing how a CEO can leverage vanity to market themselves and their company on a global scale.

THE POWER OF VANITY IN ENTREPRENEURSHIP

Vanity, when channeled appropriately, fuels the drive to be seen, admired, and respected. For an entrepreneur, this desire can translate into a relentless pursuit of visibility and recognition, which are critical components of effective marketing and PR. Vanity pushes entrepreneurs to showcase their achievements, highlight their unique qualities, and position themselves as thought leaders in their industry.

Personal Branding: The First Step

The concept of personal branding revolves around the idea of marketing oneself. It is about creating a distinctive image and reputation that sets an individual apart from others. For entrepreneurs, personal branding is not just about self-promotion; it is a strategic approach to gaining credibility, attracting opportunities, and building a loyal following.

Crafting Your Personal Brand

❶ IDENTIFY YOUR UNIQUE SELLING PROPOSITION (USP)

Every successful brand has a USP, and personal branding is no different. Entrepreneurs need to identify what makes them unique. Is it their innovative thinking, their industry expertise, or their charismatic leadership? Understanding and articulating this USP is the foundation of a strong personal brand.

❷ CONSISTENT MESSAGING

Consistency is key in personal branding. Entrepreneurs should ensure that their messaging across all platforms—social media, interviews, public speaking engagements—aligns with their brand identity. This includes their tone of voice, visual style, and core values.

❸ AUTHENTICITY

Authenticity resonates with audiences. Entrepreneurs should embrace their true selves and share their genuine stories. Authenticity builds trust and fosters deeper connections with the audience.

❹ VISIBILITY

An essential aspect of personal branding is visibility. Entrepreneurs should actively seek opportunities to be seen and heard. This includes participating in industry events, speaking at conferences, writing articles, and engaging with the media.

VANITY IN PR AND MARKETING

Vanity drives entrepreneurs to seek recognition, and PR and marketing are the vehicles through which this recognition is achieved. PR and marketing amplify an entrepreneur's presence, making their personal brand and their company known to a wider audience.

The Role of PR

Public Relations (PR) is about managing the flow of information between an individual or an organization and the public. For entrepreneurs, PR is crucial in shaping public perception, building a positive image, and managing their reputation.

❶ MEDIA RELATIONS

Building strong relationships with media outlets is essential. Entrepreneurs should aim to be featured in influential publications, on television, and on digital platforms. This not only enhances visibility but also positions them as industry experts.

❷ PRESS RELEASES AND ANNOUNCEMENTS

Regularly issuing press releases about company milestones, product launches, and other significant events keeps the public informed and engaged. It also creates a sense of dynamism and progress around the entrepreneur and their business.

CRISIS MANAGEMENT

Vanity can be a double-edged sword. While it drives entrepreneurs to seek recognition, it also means they are under constant scrutiny. Effective PR strategies include crisis management plans to handle any negative publicity or challenges that may arise.

The Role of Marketing

Marketing is about promoting products or services to target audiences. For entrepreneurs, marketing is essential in reaching potential customers, generating leads, and driving sales.

CONTENT MARKETING

Creating valuable and relevant content positions entrepreneurs as thought leaders and keeps their audience engaged. This includes blog posts, videos, podcasts, and social media content.

SOCIAL MEDIA MARKETING

Social media platforms are powerful tools for entrepreneurs to showcase their personality, engage with their audience, and promote their brand. Consistent and strategic social media activity can significantly enhance an entrepreneur's visibility and influence.

INFLUENCER PARTNERSHIPS

Collaborating with influencers who align with the entrepreneur's brand can extend reach and credibility. Influencers can help promote products, services, and even the entrepreneur's personal brand to a wider audience.

ADVERTISING

Investing in advertising, whether digital or traditional, can amplify an entrepreneur's reach. Targeted advertising ensures that the message reaches the right audience, increasing the likelihood of engagement and conversion.

CASE STUDIES: VANITY IN ACTION

Elon Musk: The Epitome of Personal Branding

Elon Musk is a prime example of how vanity, when channeled effectively, can lead to unprecedented success. Musk's personal brand is inseparable from his ventures—Tesla, SpaceX, Neuralink, and the Boring Company. His charisma, bold vision, and willingness to engage with the public have made him a household name. Musk's vanity drives him to constantly be in the spotlight, whether through tweets, public appearances, or controversial statements. This relentless pursuit of visibility has not only elevated his personal brand but also brought immense attention to his companies. Tesla's marketing budget is significantly lower than its competitors, yet it enjoys unparalleled media coverage and public interest, largely due to Musk's personal branding efforts.

Oprah Winfrey: Building an Empire on Authenticity

Oprah Winfrey's journey from a talk show host to a global media mogul is a testament to the power of authenticity in personal branding. Winfrey's genuine personality, coupled with her compelling storytelling, has built a deep connection with her audience. Winfrey's vanity lies in her desire to positively impact the world, which she has achieved through her media empire, philanthropic efforts, and personal brand. Her authenticity and willingness to share her personal experiences have made her a trusted and beloved figure, resulting in a loyal following and immense influence.

Richard Branson: The Adventurous Entrepreneur

Richard Branson, founder of Virgin Group, is known for his adventurous spirit and flamboyant personality. Branson's vanity drives him to take risks, challenge the status quo, and constantly seek the limelight. Branson's personal brand is characterized by his adventurous endeavors, from attempting to circumnavigate the globe in a hot air balloon to his ventures into space tourism with Virgin Galactic. His willingness to put himself at the forefront of his brand has created a strong association between his personality and his businesses, enhancing their visibility and appeal.

THE CEO AS THE FACE OF THE COMPANY

In today's business landscape, the CEO is often seen as the face of the company. Their actions, personality, and public image can significantly impact the company's reputation and success. Vanity, when harnessed correctly, can help CEOs effectively market themselves and their companies.

Building Trust and Credibility

A CEO who is visible and actively engaged with the public can build trust and credibility. When customers see a CEO who is passionate, knowledgeable, and approachable, they are more likely to trust the company and its products.

❶ TRANSPARENCY

Being open and transparent about the company's goals, challenges, and achievements fosters trust. Regularly communicating with stakeholders through interviews, social media, and public statements builds credibility.

✿ THOUGHT LEADERSHIP

Sharing insights and expertise positions the CEO as a thought leader in the industry. This can be achieved through speaking engagements, writing articles, and participating in industry panels.

Humanizing the Brand

A CEO who is actively involved in marketing and PR efforts can humanize the brand. Customers are more likely to connect with a company that has a relatable and charismatic leader.

✿ STORYTELLING

Sharing personal stories and experiences can create an emotional connection with the audience. This makes the brand more relatable and memorable.

✿ ENGAGEMENT

Actively engaging with customers, whether through social media interactions or public events, shows that the CEO values their audience. This fosters loyalty and strengthens the brand's community.

Driving Media Coverage

A CEO who actively markets themselves can attract significant media coverage. Media outlets are drawn to charismatic and influential leaders, which can result in extensive coverage of both the CEO and the company.

✿ INTERVIEWS AND FEATURES

Participating in interviews and being featured in prominent publications enhances the CEO's and the company's visibility. This can lead to increased brand awareness and credibility.

⚙ PUBLIC SPEAKING

Speaking at conferences, industry events, and public forums positions the CEO as a leader and innovator. This not only enhances their personal brand but also brings attention to the company.

INVESTING IN PR AND MARKETING: A STRATEGIC IMPERATIVE

For entrepreneurs, investing in PR and marketing is not just an option; it is a strategic imperative. Vanity, when harnessed correctly, can drive entrepreneurs to invest in building a strong personal brand and effectively marketing themselves and their companies.

The ROI of PR and Marketing

Investing in PR and marketing yields significant returns in terms of visibility, credibility, and growth. A strong personal brand and effective marketing strategies can attract investors, partners, customers, and media attention.

⚙ VISIBILITY

Increased visibility leads to greater brand recognition and awareness. This can result in higher customer acquisition and retention rates.

⚙ CREDIBILITY

Effective PR and marketing efforts build credibility and trust. This enhances the company's reputation and can lead to more business opportunities.

✿ GROWTH

A strong personal brand and effective marketing strategies drive growth by attracting new customers, expanding market reach, and fostering loyalty.

The Cost of Neglecting PR and Marketing

Neglecting PR and marketing can have detrimental effects on an entrepreneur's success. Without visibility and credibility, even the most innovative products and services can struggle to gain traction.

❶ LACK OF AWARENESS

Without effective marketing, potential customers may not even be aware of the company's existence. This can result in missed opportunities and stagnation.

❷ LOSS OF TRUST

In today's transparent and connected world, a lack of engagement and transparency can lead to a loss of trust. This can damage the company's reputation and hinder growth.

❸ MISSED OPPORTUNITIES

Neglecting PR and marketing can result in missed opportunities for media coverage, partnerships, and business growth. This can limit the company's potential and hinder its success.

Vanity, when channeled appropriately, can be a powerful driver of entrepreneurial success. It fuels the desire for visibility, recognition, and influence, which are critical components of effective PR and marketing. By embracing vanity, entrepreneurs can build strong personal brands, engage with a global audience, and position their companies for unparalleled success. Investing in PR and marketing is not just about self-promotion; it is a strategic approach to building credibility, attracting opportunities, and driving growth. The CEO, as the face of the company, plays a crucial role in this process. Their actions, personality, and public image can significantly impact the company's reputation and success.

In today's competitive business landscape, embracing vanity and investing in PR and marketing are not just options; they are strategic imperatives for entrepreneurial success. So let vanity be your favorite sin, and watch as it propels you and your company to new heights of recognition and success.

CHAPTER 32

REINCARNATION

In the world of entrepreneurship, the journey of a startup founder can often feel like an endless cycle of birth, death, and rebirth—much like the concept of reincarnation. Just as in life, where one must sometimes accept the end of one chapter to embrace a new beginning, startup founders must recognize when it's time to stop trying with their current venture and pivot, sell, or even completely start anew. This process requires not just determination and grit, but also wisdom and self-awareness to understand when perseverance transforms into stubbornness. In this chapter, we will explore the metaphor of reincarnation in the startup world and how founders can master the art of knowing when to let go and move forward.

THE CONCEPT OF REINCARNATION IN ENTREPRENEURSHIP

Reincarnation, in spiritual and philosophical contexts, refers to the belief that after death, the soul is reborn in a new body. This cycle continues until the soul reaches enlightenment or liberation. In the context of startups, reincarnation can be seen as the cycle of creation, failure, and rebirth. Each new venture a founder undertakes is like a new incarnation, shaped by the experiences and lessons learned from previous attempts. Startup founders are often driven by a vision and a passion to create something impactful. However, not every idea will succeed, and not every venture will reach its desired outcome. Accepting failure and learning from it is a crucial part of the entrepreneurial journey. Just as the soul carries forward its learnings into each new life, founders must carry forward their insights and experiences into each new venture.

The First Incarnation: The Birth of a Startup

The journey of a startup begins with an idea—a spark of inspiration that ignites the founder's passion. This phase is characterized by excitement, energy, and optimism. Founders pour their heart and soul into developing their product or service, building a team, and launching their venture. This is the honeymoon phase, where everything seems possible. However, as the startup progresses, challenges begin to surface. Market dynamics, competition, funding issues, and operational hurdles can all pose significant threats to the fledgling venture. It is during these times that the founder's resilience and adaptability are tested. The key is to remain open to feedback and be willing to make necessary changes.

The Struggles and Signs of Decline

Every startup faces struggles, but there comes a point when the challenges seem insurmountable. Sales may stagnate, customer acquisition costs might skyrocket, or the market simply may not respond as expected. It is crucial for founders to recognize the signs of decline. Ignoring these signs can lead to prolonged suffering and wasted resources. Signs of decline can include the following:

1. Consistently missing key performance metrics

2. Negative cash flow without a clear path to profitability

3. High churn rates and declining customer satisfaction

4. Inability to raise additional funding

5. Team morale plummeting

Recognizing these signs early allows founders to take proactive measures rather than being forced into reactive decisions later.

The Pivotal Decision: To Pivot or Not

When a startup faces significant challenges, one of the first options to consider is a pivot. A pivot involves changing the business model, target market, or product offering based on new insights or market conditions. Successful pivots can breathe new life into a struggling startup and set it on a path to success. A famous example of a successful pivot is X (formerly Twitter). Originally launched as Odeo, a platform for podcasting, the founders realized that the podcasting market was not growing as expected. They pivoted to focus on a microblogging service, which eventually became Twitter, and then X as we know it today. To decide whether to pivot, founders should consider the following:

▶ Customer Feedback: Is there a consistent theme in customer feedback that suggests a different approach?

▶ Market Trends: Are there emerging trends or gaps in the market that the startup can address?

▶ Team Capabilities: Does the team have the skills and resources to execute the pivot?

▶ Financial Health: Does the startup have enough runway to make the pivot and sustain itself during the transition?

If the answer to these questions is affirmative, a pivot might be a viable option. However, it's important to approach a pivot with a clear plan and a willingness to experiment and iterate.

Considering a Sale or Acqui-Hire

If a pivot doesn't seem feasible or the startup continues to struggle despite multiple attempts at course correction, founders might consider selling the company or pursuing an acqui-hire. Selling the company involves finding a buyer who sees value in the startup's assets, technology, or market presence. An acqui-hire, on the other hand, involves selling the company primarily for the talent and expertise of its team. Selling the startup can be a difficult decision, as it often feels like admitting defeat. However, it's important to recognize that selling can be a strategic move that provides value to stakeholders and offers a new beginning for the founder and the team. To pursue a sale or acqui-hire, founders should do the following:

- ▶ Identify Potential Buyers: Look for companies that could benefit from the startup's technology, market presence, or team.

- ▶ Prepare Financials and Valuation: Ensure that the company's financials are in order, and obtain a realistic valuation.

- ▶ Engage Advisors: Work with advisors or brokers who can facilitate the sale process.

- ▶ Negotiate Terms: Focus on securing favorable terms that protect the interests of the team and stakeholders.

The End of a Chapter: Shutting Down and Reflecting

In some cases, a pivot or sale may not be possible, and the best option is to shut down the startup. This is often the hardest decision for founders to make, as it feels like the end of a dream. However, shutting down with grace and integrity can set the stage for future success. Here's what shutting down involves:

▶ Communicating Transparently: Inform stakeholders, investors, customers, and employees about the decision and the reasons behind it.

▶ Closing Financials: Settle outstanding debts, pay off liabilities, and ensure that all financial matters are resolved.

▶ Reflecting and Learning: Take time to reflect on what went wrong and what could have been done differently. This introspection is crucial for personal and professional growth.

The Rebirth: Starting Anew

Just as reincarnation brings the soul into a new life with the wisdom of past experiences, the end of one startup can be the beginning of a new venture for the founder. The lessons learned from previous failures become invaluable assets in the next journey. Starting anew involves these steps:

▶ Assessing the Market: Identify new opportunities and gaps in the market that align with the founder's vision and expertise.

▶ Building on Strengths: Leverage the skills, knowledge, and networks gained from the previous venture.

- ▶ Embracing a Growth Mindset: Approach the new venture with a mindset of continuous learning and improvement.

Many successful entrepreneurs have experienced multiple failures before achieving significant success. For example, Elon Musk faced numerous challenges with his early ventures before achieving success with companies like SpaceX and Tesla.

The Wisdom to Know When to Let Go

The key to successful reincarnation in the startup world lies in the wisdom to know when to let go. Perseverance is a valuable trait, but so is the ability to recognize when a venture is no longer viable. This wisdom comes from self-awareness, humility, and a willingness to seek advice and feedback from trusted mentors and advisors.

Embracing Failure as a Stepping Stone

Failure is often stigmatized, but in the entrepreneurial world, it should be embraced as a stepping stone to success. Each failure provides valuable insights and experiences that shape the founder's journey. Here are some benefits of embracing failure:

- ▶ Learning from Mistakes: Analyze what went wrong and identify key lessons.

- ▶ Resilience and Adaptability: Develop the resilience to bounce back and the adaptability to navigate future challenges.

- ▶ Maintaining Optimism: Keep a positive outlook and believe in the potential for future success.

The Role of Mentorship and Support Networks

Navigating the cycles of reincarnation in the startup world is not a journey that founders should undertake alone. Mentorship and support networks play a crucial role in providing guidance, encouragement, and perspective. Experienced mentors can help founders identify when it's time to pivot, sell, or shut down, and support networks can provide emotional and practical support during difficult times.

The journey of a startup founder is a continuous cycle of birth, death, and rebirth. Each incarnation brings new challenges and opportunities for growth. The key to mastering this cycle lies in the wisdom to know when to let go and the courage to start anew. By embracing the concept of reincarnation, startup founders can navigate their journeys with resilience, adaptability, and a relentless pursuit of their dreams. In the end, the genius of entrepreneurship lies not just in creating and building, but also in knowing when to stop trying with one venture and pivot, sell, or start anew with another. This cycle of reincarnation is what ultimately leads to the fulfillment of the founder's vision and the creation of lasting impact.